WITHDRAWN

Streams for the Future?

The long term effects of
early streaming and non-streaming
—the final report of the
Banbury Grouping Enquiry

First Published March 1978

by Pubansco.

ISBN 0-9504302-1-8.

Printed by Smart & Co. (Printers) Ltd. 19a, Manor Road, Brackley, Northants.

Foreword

This volume from Banbury School is unusually important. Firstly, it is an instance of research initiated by a school calling in the expertise and experience of established national bodies, advisers, and Her Majesty's Inspectorate to guide and support it, and securing from industry and government a lifeline budget to complete its tasks. It is, then, a prime example of school-focussed enquiry.

Secondly, it answers the questions about groupings in the early years of secondary schooling to which society wants urgent answers: what are the long-term effects?

Its findings are the closest we have as yet to an answer for the whole country.

Thirdly, its findings are in the main reassuring to teachers and others concerned, and should end some of the wild generalisations which have been permitted for want of evidence.

Finally, the evidence on subject choice shows a pronounced change between sciences and languages, according to the previous grouping, and especially among girls of middling ability.

With this report, the present partnership of the staff of Banbury School, the National Foundation for Educational Research, and the Oxford Department of Educational Studies, with the Advisory Service of Oxfordshire and Her Majesty's Inspectorate is concluded. We hope that it will inspire many similar shared projects.

Alfred Yates
Director, N.F.E.R.

John Sayer
Principal, Banbury School.

Preface

Although mixed ability teaching groups have been a feature of secondary schools for many years, their desirability is still a matter which raises a great deal of interest and not a small amount of controversy. The questions are complicated by the fact that the debate is usually conducted on the basis of personal conviction, political bias or the current trend in educational fashion. There is a very real lack of reliable, quantitative information, particularly that gathered under controlled conditions in this country. It is perhaps indicative of the scarcity of this sort of evidence that the Institute of Physics has recently called upon the Department of Education and Science to undertake a study and to place a moratorium on the further introduction of mixed ability grouping until the results are known.[1]

The work of the Banbury Grouping Project is intended to go some way to filling this gap. A first phase of the Project has already reported to the D.E.S. and its work has been published by N.F.E.R.[2] It collected a great deal of background information on approximately one thousand students at Banbury School. The main groups of students who were studied, were followed through their first two years of secondary education, and the analyses carried out by Phase One give, therefore, an insight into the effects of mixed ability groupings on young people aged 11 to 13. It has been the work of this second phase to follow these same pupils through to the end of their fifth year and therefore to complete the study of the impact of early grouping systems on the whole of the compulsory secondary education process.

Before proceeding with a detailed discussion of the work of Phase Two, the authors would like to acknowledge their indebtedness to Dr. D. E. Newbold, who was Research Officer during Phase One, for the bank of background data which he collected, to Mr. J. K. Backhouse of the Department of Educational Studies, Oxford University, for his advice and help in the fields of statistics and computing, and to Dr. B. Phelps of the Oxford University Computing Service. Our thanks are also due to Mr. K. Palmer, Director of Studies at Banbury School, for many hours of useful discussion and much practical assistance, to our long-suffering colleagues at Banbury and Drayton Schools and, especially, to our wives for their help and encouragement.

---

[1] Times Educational Supplement 8 July 1977
[2] David Newbold *Ability Grouping, the Banbury Enquiry*—N.F.E.R. Publishing Co. 1977

2

Contents

Introduction

Since a comprehensive review of the literature on this subject was given by Dr. Newbold in the report on the first phase of the Banbury Grouping Enquiry, we will not present such a review in this document.

We therefore begin this chapter with a description of those aspects of the organisation of Banbury School which are relevant to a full understanding of the research. We then present an outline of the research programme and give, in summary, the main findings of the first phase. Subsequent chapters give detailed accounts of the individual areas of study which formed the second phase. Chapter 8 is intended to help the reader who does not have a detailed knowledge of statistics to understand the terms and techniques used in these chapters. The final chapter attempts to relate the results obtained in each of these separate areas to the general hypotheses which Phase Two was designed to test. Throughout the report the figures presented in the text are augmented by additional information in the appendices. These should be consulted for basic data, repetitive analyses and additional statistics which we felt did not merit space in the main body of the report.

1.1 BANBURY SCHOOL

Over the years during which the research programme has been under way, Banbury School has been through several changes. It has, however, maintained the federal structure which is fundamental to the research design. (This structure, however, was not established for the purposes of research but rather as a way of running a very large school in units which were small enough to provide the pupils, and indeed the staff, with a sense of belonging, and contributing, to a community in which individuals were important.) Pupils, when they enter the school, join one of a number of halls. They stay in this same hall for their first four years and, for the first three years anyway, have most of their lessons in their hall with teachers who are themselves based in that hall. Each of the halls is geographically separate and, to a very large extent, feels itself to be independent. At the end of their fourth year the pupils transfer to the Upper School which provides the fifth, sixth and seventh year courses for pupils from all of the halls.

Teachers, when they join the school, are also based in a hall or in the Upper School. They do much of their teaching in this home base although most of the Upper School staff teach some hall-based classes and many hall-based teachers share in the work of the Upper School. Hall staffs, while retaining some of the autonomy which is felt by pupils in the halls, are more aware of the school as a whole, for there are regular departmental meetings involving those from all communities who teach a particular subject, and departmental policy, decided at such meetings, is implemented by a single Head of Department, across the whole of Banbury School.

This structure of distinctive units working to the same ends makes Banbury School an ideal setting for research as one can change certain factors in one or more of the halls and then compare the performance of the halls as they each strive for the common goal. The Banbury Grouping Project has exploited precisely this feature of the federal structure in order to compare two systems of grouping in secondary schools. Such exploitation was not, however, the result of a Machiavellian plot. It proved possible because of a lack of certainty within the school as to whether or not mixed ability teaching was desirable in the first few years of secondary schooling. This resulted in the school's own decision that some halls would adopt mixed ability groupings while others would continue with the streaming system which had been running up to that time. It was only after this fundamental decision was made at a school level that the Project was designed, and the details of the proposal worked out to improve the validity of any findings which might arise from it. Amongst these details were :

   (i)   the opportunity for staff to move into a Hall with a particular grouping system if they felt strongly that they would prefer to work in one system rather than the other.

   (ii)   the careful balancing of the pupils allocated to each Hall so that the samples involved in each system were of equal ability. (This had always been part of the usual admissions procedure and the checks carried out by the first phase of the research were an indication of how successfully this had been done).

   (iii)   the careful matching of pupils according to social criteria. (Since primary schools have very limited catchment areas within the town, and therefore tend to have a restricted range of socio-economic groups represented within their pupil populations, this social matching between two systems of grouping can only be achieved in a federal secondary school where pupils from each primary school can be divided between the communities under study).

   (iv)   the adoption of only two grouping systems, despite the fact that there were at that time four halls, so that analyses could be made *within* a given system as well as *between* the two different systems.

It might be argued that this basic research design has two weaknesses: first, that research based on just one school, however large, is bound to be of limited value in the broader context of schools nationwide, and secondly, that it is perhaps inappropriate that the aims of a mixed ability community should be so closely akin to those of a streamed community and that we might therefore be assessing the extent to which mixed ability teaching can achieve aims for which it was never really designed. Whilst accepting that these are points which should be borne in mind as this report is read, we nevertheless feel that a study done in one establishment, with systems working towards one set of aims, avoids so many of the imponderables which exist in comparisons between different schools (factors such as differences in physical and human resources, differences of curricular emphasis, differences of ethos and expectation etc.) that its results are more likely to be valid and therefore *more* likely to be of use outside the walls of the school involved, than are those of the 'inter-school' type of enquiry. In addition we feel that it is important to note that, despite its unusual structure, Banbury School is very much a 'main stream' establishment, involved in most of the things which other schools are doing and working to aims which most schools would recognise as similar to their own. Extrapolation of well validated results from this fairly standard situation should not lead to too many errors. Again, this middle ground which Banbury holds, provides an answer to the second point of concern. Banbury's aims may not be exactly those for which the mixed ability grouping system's strongest advocates would choose to work. They are, however, the aims for which most schools work and so, differences reported here between one grouping system and another, are differences which schools elsewhere will wish to bear in mind when decisions on grouping are being made. We leave to others the interesting and important task of assessing the grouping systems in terms of their success in achieving some of the more progressive aims in education.

We move now to a brief description of the curricular structure of Banbury School. For the first three years, pupils in all Halls follow an identical curriculum which does not permit any choice on their part (except in the area of languages where, at the time at which the pupils under study were involved, a second foreign language could be taken up outside the normal timetable if they wished to do so). The full details of this curriculum showing the balance between subjects is given in Appendix 1. Towards the end of the Spring term of a pupil's third year, teachers produce a prognosis of his potential for success in examinations at the end of year five. On the basis of these prognoses and of discussion with pupils and parents, tutors counsel third formers to help them make sensible choices of fourth year subjects. Within the limits set down by the prognoses, and certain general guiding principles (e.g. all pupils must study at least one science) third formers are free to choose seven of their fourth year subjects from the offer of subjects made in the 'Grid'. All continue a study of Maths and English and follow a Core programme (which provides Music, Library, Careers, PE and Health Education lessons), in addition to the seven freely chosen subjects. The full details of the grid offer and of the constraints placed upon free choice are given in Appendix 2. This individual programme of study is continued by most pupils without further opportunity for change until the end of year five. Some however, on transfer to the Upper School opt to continue their education in the Berrymoor Unit rather than the main Upper School building. This unit is adjacent to the local technical college and, through close links with that establishment, aims to provide its students with courses with greater vocational bias than is possible in the Upper School. These pupils will change some of their academic fourth year subjects for vocational ones at this fifth year stage. All pupils, at the end of year five, can consider the possibility of continuing to years six and seven. If they choose to do so, a course choice procedure which is very similar to that in year three, but with fewer constraints, is followed.

Finally it is necessary to identify the halls and to describe in greater detail the grouping systems employed in them. At the same time we will outline the changes which have occurred over the years of the study, for one of these has provided the research with an interesting opportunity. At the time when the study began there were four lower halls in Banbury School; they are listed below with a record of the grouping systems which were in operation. Grimsbury Hall, which was off the main site, moved into new buildings to the north west of Banbury in 1973, and became Drayton Hall. At this time it changed its grouping system for new entrants to exploit the opportunities offered by its new environment. Drayton Hall became a separate school in 1975 but it has proved possible to continue to include it in the study.

Table 1.1   Grouping Systems in use in the Halls

Hall	Grouping System
Broughton	Mixed Ability
Wykham	Mixed Ability
Stanbridge	Streamed
⎰Grimsbury	Streamed (1972 and earlier intakes)
⎱Drayton	Mixed Ability (1973 and later intakes)

The 1972 intake (Cohort 3) is the subject of much of the work of Phase One and is, almost exclusively, the subject of Phase Two. Because of the change in grouping system at Grimsbury/Drayton, their 1973 intake (Cohort 4) has been included and will be discussed later, particularly in the chapter on subject choice.

We feel that it is most important for a proper understanding of the scope and limitations of this project that the exact application of the terms 'mixed abiliy' and 'streaming' to the Banbury situation is made clear.

First the terms apply only to the grouping system used in the first year teaching groups. Wykham Hall remains predominantly mixed ability for year two whereas Broughton is mainly streamed in year two. Both are largely streamed or setted (i.e. grouped by departments, on the basis of ability in a given subject) in the teaching groups used in year three. Stanbridge and Drayton (for Cohort 3) adopt streamed teaching groups up to year three.

All halls adopt mixed ability tutor groups, for pastoral purposes only, in year four. Fourth year teaching groups are partly decided by the option system outlined above and partly, as in year three, by departmental setting. This implies that any *differences between systems detected by this research are differences occurring as a result of different grouping systems in pupils' first years in the secondary school* and not as a result of different systems throughout their secondary schooling. This may tend to weaken the magnitude of any effects and may obscure some differences which might be revealed in a study that involved longer term exposure to mixed ability groupings. It does however make the findings particularly relevant to schools which, while wishing to adopt mixed ability teaching at some levels, fight shy of introducing it for all pupils, especially those in the last stages of preparation for public examinations.

Secondly, the exact nature of the groupings must be specified. The Banbury School pupils whom we studied were of all abilities from remedial (though not E.S.N.) to 'high fliers'. In the mixed ability halls this same range is also present in each of the first year teaching groups. In the streamed halls the pupils are divided into four streams on the basis of primary school estimates so that approximately the top 25% form one teaching group, the middle 55% form two parallel middle stream groups and the least able 20% form the lowest stream teaching group. This is a fairly rough form of streaming (the top stream being wider in ability than an entire grammar school intake would have been). Again, differences between systems will tend to be weakened and those which do emerge are therefore to be dismissed only after very careful consideration. Banbury School was, at the time of entry of the students who have been most carefully studied, the only secondary school in the area (other than a small Roman Catholic school). Its intake was drawn, therefore, from the town and its surrounding villages and thus represented a good cross section of the whole range of socio-economic groups. (In this respect it is important to note that Banbury has overspill housing from Birmingham and London.) This unusual completeness of representation of both the academic and social spectrum is not significantly affected by withdrawal of pupils to the independent sector of education. Full details of the 1972 (Cohort 3) and 1973 (Cohort 4) intakes including a comparison of the way in which they were distributed between the halls can be found in the Report on Phase One. The key tables are given here in Appendix 3.

1.2 RESEARCH STRUCTURE

The research has fallen into two distinct phases both of which were funded by the D.E.S. and guided by the Department of Educational Studies at Oxford University together with the National Foundation for Educational Research. Phase One was conducted by a full time research officer aided by a research assistant. Phase Two has been more closely school based. It has been run by two members of staff from Banbury School who, between them, have been able to devote six tenths of one man's time to the research. There was a period of one year between the end of phase one and the formal beginning of phase two. A certain amount of work was made possible during this period partly as a result of a grant of money from British Petroleum.

1.2.1 The terms of reference of the first phase were 'to examine the differences, social and academic, which arise in the early years of secondary education from two systems of ability grouping, homogeneous and heterogeneous, within a single controlled situation'. It was launched as an open ended investigation without the formulation of precise hypotheses which were to be tested. It developed into a predominantly statistical survey and became therefore an objective comparison of overall differences rather than a compilation of detailed individual case studies. To preserve statistical validity it was felt that the research should not feed back its results quickly into the consciousness of the school. The Project was indeed at pains to point out the differences between its style of objective assessment and the action research which would have had such feedback as a central part of its philosophy.

The findings were reported to the D.E.S. in Autumn 1975 and in the Autumn of 1977 an abbreviated version was published by N.F.E.R.[1] A necessarily brief statement of these findings is given below. It is important to mention that the inevitable process of selection has been carried through with the particular needs of the reader of this report in mind and that what follows can in no way be taken as an adequate record of the work which was carried on during phase one.

Phase One showed that, in the 11-13 age range, the relative effects of different grouping systems on academic progress were small compared with other factors. There seemed to be no evidence of under-achievement on the part of high VRQ pupils and there did seem to be some support for the view that lower ability pupils achieved higher standards when taught in mixed ability groups. Middle ability pupils especially, but all others as well to a lesser extent, scored higher on fluency and flexibility tests if taught in the mixed ability situation.

Different primary school backgrounds were shown clearly to influence pupil achievement in year one though the effect was smaller in years two and above. It was particularly noted that the pattern of primary school estimates of ability (the basis of allocation to streams in the streamed system) varied significantly between one primary school and the next. This was seen to be a major problem in the fair allocation of pupils from a variety of primary schools to their correct stream. It was noted that primary schools tended to underestimate the abilities of their highest VRQ pupils.

Friendship patterns were examined and it was shown that, in the mixed ability situation friendship choices were less often limited to pupils of similar social class and academic ability.

The study has shown that some differences in pupils attitudes emerge in the 11-13 age range as a consequence of different systems of grouping. In particular, it was shown that less able pupils were more content with their form placement in the mixed ability system. They felt happier with their class themselves, and also perceived that others held their class in higher esteem.

The study confirmed the view, long established amongst teachers, that the introduction of mixed ability teaching groups imposed a considerable strain on the staff involved. It was felt that this strain was reduced as time went on but, nevertheless, the teacher in charge of a mixed ability group was seen to be in a situation in which a successful outcome could only be achieved by the expenditure of a great deal of skill and not a little energy !

1.2.2 As Phase One drew to a close, the pupils whom it had studied most closely were in their second (Cohort 4) and third (Cohort 3) years. At this stage some were about to embark on the process of fourth year option choice and, within a short time, on the ritual of first public examinations. It was clearly inappropriate to bring the study of their school careers to an end at this moment. Phase Two was set up to continue this study and was asked to address itself to three basic questions which are stated below. It was intended that the answers to these questions would arise from the study of a wide range of data (also indicated below). In view of the smaller scale of Phase Two it was felt that this approach (many routes to a small number of objectives) would be more productive than an attempt to answer a large number of separate questions. The style of question asked was to some extent coloured by the fact that extensive additional testing would be impossible both because of the lack of research time and, perhaps more important, the fact that the pupils under study would be preparing for O-levels and CSEs and so would themselves be unable to support a full scale

---

[1] David Newbold—*op cit.*

testing programme. Phase Two was therefore designed as a project which would rely to a considerable extent on data generated in the normal course of school life and on the data bank left by Phase One. Since much of its data existed before results of analyses began to appear it was seen as appropriate to feed back results quickly within the school. This double contact with the school (the use of school generated data which teachers could trust and see as relevant to their own interests, and the quick feedback) has made it possible for Phase Two to arouse a good deal of interest, despite the fact that there had been a one year gap when little more than data collection had been going on.

The questions to which Phase Two was asked to turn its attention were :

    (i)   Do the specific effects of mixed ability grouping, which were disclosed by Phase One, continue beyond the point at which the pupils involved are being taught predominantly in a mixed ability situation?

           Relevant data—peer group and friendship patterns, levels of attainment, pupil attitudes to school.

    (ii) Are there differences between the types of choice made by pupils from different grouping backgrounds?

           Relevant data—personal subject preference, career aspiration, actual subject choice, aspiration for continued education, involvement in school.

    (iii) Are there differences in the way in which pupils are advised by their counsellors and form teachers if they are taught in different grouping systems

           Relevant data—correlation of prognosis and achievement, course satisfaction.

In so far as Phase Two is concerned with effects made apparent by Phase One, its methods are inevitably similar; it is therefore a statistical survey which has relied to a large extent on computer analysis of data. Programmes for the analysis have largely been written by the researchers although some use of standard packages (e.g. SPSS) and of programmes written by Mr. J. K. Backhouse of the Oxford University Department of Educational Studies has been made. Since its data existed at a very early stage the quick feedback of results mentioned above was considered to be in order (i.e. there would be no lowering of statistical validity by change of expectation influencing subsequent measurement). It has been seen as an important aspect of the work of Phase Two that it should where possible adjust, and in particular extend, its analysis to help other members of staff (e.g. Heads of Departments, Careers Staff and Counsellors) in the fulfilment of their own roles. To this end members of staff have played an important role in the Steering Group which has guided the project throughout its activities.

A study of friendship patterns

2.1 Introduction

Our aim in this chapter is to show whether differences between friendship patterns of pupils from streamed and mixed ability grouping systems continued to show up in the fourth year of secondary schooling (by which time all of the pupils under study would have been in similar teaching and pastoral systems).

The findings can be summarised as follows :

   (i)   a higher proportion of early friendships survived into the fourth year if pupils started their school life in a streamed system of grouping.

  (ii)   if all friendship groups which existed at fourth year level were studied no significant differences could be detected between the patterns of choice for pupils from streamed and mixed ability backgrounds.

 (iii)   if only those friendships which survived from the first or second year were studied, it was apparent that there was a greater tendency for pupils from a streamed background to choose friends of similar verbal reasoning quotient (VRQ).

  (iv)   in these 'surviving friendships', there was also a greater tendency for pupils from the streamed systems to have, as friends, pupils with similar scores on tests which measure levels of anxiety in the classroom and overall academic self-image.

2.2 Collection of Data

The main data used in this study is, of course, information on friendship choices which are made in pupils' fourth year. It has been the aim of the second phase of the project to use school generated data as far as possible rather than to collect data specifically for the purposes of research. This policy gives rise to some difficulties but has the enormous advantage that the data is more likely to be familiar to teachers in the schools. This second point is of great importance when one comes to the stage of reporting back to teachers and of involving them in plans for extension work. Both of these considerations were seen to be of crucial importance for a school-based research project.

In the work on friendship patterns, such school generated data was available for all pupils except those choosing to go to Berrymoor[1] for their fifth year (95 of the 347 pupils involved). Pupils who move into the Upper School are assigned to tutor groups for pastoral and administrative purposes. Before their transfer they are asked to give the names of friends so that friendship groupings can be preserved. Since tutor groups are never teaching groups and since each tutor group consists of pupils from each of the contributory halls, there are no artificial constraints on the friendship choices which can be incorporated into any one tutor group. Since also, pupils have a very real vested interest in giving the names of genuine friends we feel sure that the data collected reflects closely the whole range of friendship choice existing in the school.[2]

---

[1] The place of Berrymoor in the structure of Banbury School is explained in Section 3.5.

[2] A disadvantage of this method was that we were unable to keep track of "choosers" and "chosen"; something that was possible in the questionnaire approach used in Phase One. This accounts for the fact that the tables which we have used (Table 2.4 and Appendix 4) are symmetrical.

11

Friendship patterns for pupils at Drayton School which has its own self contained fifth year and therefore does not need to ask about friendship, were established by direct questioning of pupils. It is the feeling of those who collected the data here, that only in very rare cases were pupils cautious of stating genuine friendship links.

Friendship patterns at Berrymoor have not been incorporated into the analysis because comparisons would only make sense within the Berrymoor community and this is so small that few statistical procedures could be applied to the subgroups within it. There is also the additional complication of the closeness of the link between Berrymoor and the North Oxfordshire Technical College with the consequent broadening of the opportunities for the formation of friendships from a much larger group of people.

Other data used in the friendship study has been drawn from the data bank provided by the first phase of the project. This data consists of early friendship choice (established by questionnaire in year one and year two), VRQ (measured by means of 'Verbal Test EF' set at the end of the pupils' first year), Socio-Economic Group (measured on the usual Registrar General[1] scale), Primary School of Origin, and Attitude (measured at the beginning of the pupils' secondary school career on the scale developed by NFER and used in the Barker Lunn study, 'Streaming in the Primary School').

It has been a matter of some concern that these early measures of attitude form such a major part of the comparison of friendship formation at fourth year level. This is so because we specifically set out to follow through the results of Phase One of the project which studied friendship formation in terms of the three major factors (General Attitude to School, Opinion of own school class and Anxiety and Academic Self Image) which it identified in the Barker Lunn scales. No test appropriate to the fifth year pupils, could be found to assess anxiety (other than psychological tests which would have to be administered individually and which anyway were inappropriate for most of the pupils) and since there is no 'class' as such beyond year three, no test could be used to find attitudes to it!

We have made an attempt to assess general attitudes to school in the fifth year by using NFER 'Amount of Social Interaction' (ASI)[2] tests. Any relevance of this work to a study of friendship patterns is reported together with the results from the study of the earlier attitude scales. However, it remains true that if we are to follow up all of the Phase One findings on attitudes we are left with the possibility of re-using the results from the early attitude tests . . . and no other alternative: for it would be most inappropriate to re-use the primary school based tests themselves at fifth year level.

2.3 Outline of Method

Data describing friendship groups in the fourth year was added to the main computer file for the group of pupils under study (Cohort 3 of Phase One). A programme was then written to identify which of the pairs of friends included in these groups were continuations of friendship pairs from either the first or second year of the pupils' schooling. Friendship pairs thus noted were dealt with separately in later stages of the work as they represented what might be thought of as the strong friendship pairs formed in the early years. The analysis then went forward by studying all friendship pairs and strong friendship pairs with respect to the various background criteria described in Section 2.2. This study was achieved with the help of a number of computer programmes provided by

---

[1] The Registrar General's Classification of Occupations (HMSO)

[2] Finlayson D. S., Banks O. and Loughram J. L., *Administrative Manual for Pupil Perceptions Questionnaire I (ASI).* NFER 1970

Mr. J. K. Backhouse of the Oxford University Department of Educational Studies.

The basic approach used for the analysis of results is similar to that employed in Phase One. The extent to which friends' scores on a particular test are associated is measured using the statistic Gamma.[1] Differences in the degree of association for pupils from different grouping backgrounds are then found by use of the Chi-squared test or (if numbers are small) the Fisher Exact Probability Test.

2.4 Results

2.4.1 Overall Analysis of Results

311 friendship pairs were investigated. Of these, 70 were pairs which had survived from the first or second year. The distribution of these 'strong friendships' across the three halls and Drayton School were as follows :—

Table 2.1 Proportion of strong friendships in each Hall

Hall	Strong Friends	New Friends
Broughton	6	81
Wykham	21	90
Stanbridge	21	79
Drayton	22	61

Thus, in the streamed system 30.7% of all fourth year friendships are continuations of friendships made in the early years. In the mixed ability system the proportion of strong friendships is 15.8%.

In view of this very different proportion of strong friendships in the two systems, a detailed comparison was undertaken. This comparison showed a significant difference between streamed and mixed ability systems, a significant difference between the halls in the mixed ability system but no difference between halls in the streamed system. The details of this analysis are given below :—

Table 2.2 Comparison, between and within systems, of strong and new friendships

Hall/System	Strong Friends	New Friends	Chi-Squared	Significance
Between systems				
Mixed Ability	27	144	8.99	1%
Streamed	43	97		
Within the Mixed Ability System				
Broughton	6	75	6.98	1%
Wykham	21	69		
Within the streamed System				
Stanbridge	21	58	1.04	NS
Drayton	22	39		

It is clear, then, from the percentage figures for strong friendships quoted above and, especially, from the 'between systems' section of Table 2.2, that friendships are more long lasting in the streamed grouping system.

It may be of assistance to the non-technical reader if we mention at this stage that the significance of a statistical result is a measure of the likelihood that the difference detected by the test has arisen purely as a result of chance. Thus the difference detected, is likely to arise by chance less than five times in a hundred, if the significance is 5%. Clearly the smaller the value of the percentage

---

[1] Gamma is described in *Journal of the American Statistical Association* December 1954 and June 1963.
A brief introduction to the technique is given in Chapter 8.

significance, the more likely it is that the difference under discussion is a result of something other than pure chance. A fuller discussion of this and other statistical points is given in Chapter 8. The letters 'NS' in the significance column of the tables in this report indicate that the result is Not Significant. The usual minimum level of significance which is reported is 5%, though occasionally 10% significances are noted to draw the reader's attention to some interesting trends which, while they do not reach the level which is normally regarded as statistically significant, are nevertheless worthy of closer study.

The unexpected difference between Broughton and Wykham Halls calls for some explanation. It may well be that this is the result of the method of allocation of first year pupils to forms in Wykham Hall. In this hall alone, first year forms were constructed from pupils who had attended the same primary schools. In Wykham, therefore, friendships apparent in the first year were more likely to be lasting primary school friendships. It seems that these friendships continued into the fourth year providing the greater element of stability than that which exists in Broughton where no such strong primary school links survive. This interpretation is supported by the analysis of friendship by primary school of origin, which follows (Section 2.4.2.5).

Though this explanation has the advantage of additional support from this later work on primary school of origin there is an alternative explanation. This is based on the fact that Broughton Hall regroups its classes at the beginning of year two. It may be this *lack* of continuity which reduced the number of lasting friendships in Broughton. Of course neither explanation can be *proved* from the figures quoted above. Nevertheless they do lend support to the view that stability of form grouping has a considerable influence on the stability of pupils' friendships.

In an attempt to explain why the friendships formed in the whole mixed ability system are less stable, it is tempting to make use of the fact that students in that system tend to choose friends from a wider VRQ spectrum. We might suppose that these mixed VRQ friendships are the ones which easily dissolve. We show later, in Table 2.9, that this is unlikely to be the true explanation for we are able to put forward evidence that suggests that the friendships which *do* survive in the mixed ability system are actually those same mixed VRQ friendships.

2.4.2 Analysis of Friendship Patterns by Background Criteria

2.4.2.1 Preparation of Background Data

The background data used was, with the sole exception of the ASI attitude scale results, data collected by Phase One of the project.

The first requirement of this study was to set up a system by means of which, scores on each of the background criteria could be grouped into ranges. This was done for each criterion in turn by firstly plotting a histogram of scores to ensure that the overall distribution was smooth and not bimodal. It was found that, without exception, these requirements were fulfilled by the data. The whole spread of scores was divided into ranges of equal size which were chosen so that the proportions of the population in each range were as shown in the table :

Table 2.3   Percentage of school population in each grade range

Range	1	2	3	4	5	6
% population	5	15	30	30	15	5

This method was applied directly to VRQ scores. In the case of the attitude scales, a simplifying step was taken first. Phase One had shown that in both grouping systems attitude scales A, B, C, F and G stood together as a factor expressing a pupil's overall attitude to school. Rather than handle each scale separately it was decided that we should average the scores on these five attitude scales and use this average as an indication of the pupil's overall attitude. The other factors identified in Phase One were D and E (an attitude to school class factor) and H and J (an anxiety in the classroom factor). These factors were treated in this same averaging way. It was then these three average attitude scores that were divided into ranges as described.

2.4.2.2 Analysis by VRQ

2.4.2.2a All Friendships Analysis by VRQ.

The first step in investigating the extent to which pupils choose friends of similar VRQ is to draw up a table into which each friendship pair is entered at the positions identified by the VRQs of the two pupils involved. The table for each grouping system is shown below :

Table 2.4 Association of VRQ scores for all friends

Mixed Ability System *VRQ Range*	1	2	3	4	5	6	*Streamed System* *VRQ Range*	1	2	3	4	5	6
1	0	1	0	1	0	0	1	1	5	1	2	1	0
2	1	2	8	11	3	2	2	5	3	14	11	1	3
3	0	8	4	20	14	7	3	1	14	18	25	9	11
4	1	11	20	13	13	8	4	2	11	25	15	20	9
5	0	3	14	13	9	13	5	1	1	9	20	6	19
6	0	2	7	8	13	3	6	0	3	11	9	19	3

The extent to which pupils choose friends of similar VRQ can then be assessed by measuring the degree of association using the statistic Gamma. This was done for the two tables separately and the following results obtained :

Table 2.6 Measurement of Association of Friends by VRQ

System	Gamma	Significance of Gamma
Mixed Ability	0.122	NS
Streamed	0.275	1%

We conclude that friendship choice is associated with VRQ in the streamed system and, to a far smaller extent, in the mixed ability system. In fact, the size of the association in this second case is such that we cannot be confident that it is the result of anything more than chance.

These results imply, of course, that there is a difference between the degree of association in the two systems. They do not however prove that this difference is sufficiently large to be statistically significant. In order that we might test this we drew up the following table :

Table 2.7 Comparison of association of friends by VRQ; between systems

Halls	Number choosing friends from the same VRQ range	Number choosing friends from different VRQ ranges
B+W	31	101
S+D	46	131
Chi-Squared=0.137[1] df=1 NS		

---

[1] Explanations of the chi-squared test and of the idea of degrees of freedom (df) are given in Chapter 8.

We must therefore conclude that
  (i)   friendship choice is related to VRQ in the streamed system
  (ii) the degree of association in the mixed ability system is smaller and fails to reach a significant level
  (iii) the numbers choosing friends of similar VRQ do not differ significantly between the systems.

While there is, therefore, a vestige of the Phase One result that pupils in mixed ability groups choose more widely, by the end of year four the phenomenon is not strong enough for results to reach statistical significance.

We might expect the Phase One result to hold true at year four level if only those friendships which have survived from year one or two are studied. It is to those strong friendships that we shortly turn our attention.

The remaining step in helping to establish whether or not the difference between systems, such as they are, are the result of those systems, and not of local differences in atmosphere between individual halls, was to check for differences between the halls operating the same system. We have called differences of this kind *within system* differences, while differences between Broughton and Wykham taken as a single unit, and Stanbridge and Drayton taken as the other unit, have been referred to as *between system* differences. The procedure of looking for 'within system' differences as well as 'between system' differences was one which we have frequently used and so we will digress for a moment to discuss the interpretation of these two kinds of comparison.

We feel that where the 'within system' differences were small there was evidence that the halls were not behaving in an individualistic manner. If, on the same tests, there were large 'between system' differences it would therefore be unlikely that these were simply the result of individualistic behaviour. Chance *could* of course be the explanation of such results, but we feel that it would be highly unlikely that chance alone would produce similar results in Broughton and Wykham, similar results in Stanbridge and Drayton but at the same time, large differences between the streamed system and the mixed ability system. A more natural explanation of such results is that the grouping systems were having some influence on the areas of behaviour under study. Admittedly the simplicity of such an explanation does not, in itself, constitute a proof of its accuracy, nevertheless we feel that it does imply that the explanation should be treated with some respect.

The results of these within system checks on the degree of association of friends by VRQ are given below:

Table 2.8   Comparison of Association of friends by VRQ within systems

(a) *Mixed Ability System*

Hall	Number choosing friends from the same VRQ range	Numbers choosing friends from different VRQ ranges
Broughton	14	35
Wykham	17	66

Chi-Squared=0.717 df=1   NS

(b) *Streamed System*

Hall	Number choosing friends from the same VRQ range	Numbers choosing friends from different VRQ ranges
Stanbridge	24	62
Drayton	22	69

Chi-Squared=0.155 df=1   NS

Since, in both systems, there is no significant difference between the two halls, there is no evidence that halls are displaying idiosyncratic behaviour.

2.4.2.2b Strong Friends; Analysis by VRQ

The same procedures were used for the analysis of strong friendships except that, where numbers were too small to permit the use of the chi-squared test, the Fisher Exact Probability test was used (in all cases the tables under study were 2 x 2). The results are given below :

Table 2.9   Association by VRQ; Statistical Summary; Strong friends only

	Mixed Ability System	Streamed System
Level of Association		
Gamma	—0.26	0.67
Significance of Gamma	NS	1%
Difference between halls in each system		
Fisher test	0.85	0.65
	NS	NS
Difference between systems		
Chi-Squared=4.23 df=1 5%		
(more 'similar VRQ' choices in streamed situation)		

The values of Gamma (0.67 in the streamed system and —0.26 in the mixed ability system) show that there is a far higher degree of association between the VRQs of strong friends in the streamed system. The value of Chi-Squared for the comparison between systems shows that this difference in degree of association is large enough to result in a significant difference between the numbers choosing friends of similar VRQ in the two systems. There is no evidence that halls within the same system differ significantly in this respect.

For the detailed figures from which these results were obtained, the reader is referred to Appendix 4.

2.4.2.2c Summarising Discussion

Fewer mixed ability friendships survive to year four; those which do survive (the "strong friends" in our analysis) show a far lower degree of association by VRQ than do the surviving friendships in the streamed system; the overall degree of association by VRQ for all friendships including those new ones formed in years 3 & 4 show no statistically significant difference between systems.

We feel that these results show that it is unwise to assume that the 'mixed VRQ' friendships formed in the mixed ability system are only transitory. It is also unwise to suggest that the habit of forming friends from a wider cross section of the community will continue when pupils who were initially in mixed ability groupings move into a more closely streamed environment. It would seem that the situation of the moment is the influence on whether or not 'mixed VRQ' friendships are made.

2.4.2.3 Analysis by Attitude

We have mentioned above the way in which the Barker Lunn attitude scale results of Phase One have been used in this study. The general attitude to school factor (Barker Lunn scales ABCF & G) has been extended by up to date measurements of pupil attitude using the ASI[1] scale, otherwise (for reasons stated above) all attitude data is that collected in the first year of the pupils' secondary schooling.

2.4.2.3a All Friends; Analysis by Attitudes

Throughout this section, the reader is referred to Appendix 4 for the detailed figures from which these tables were derived.

---

[1] ASI is the "Amount of Social Interaction" test referred to earlier

Table 2.10
Association of Attitude scores for all friends; Statistical Summary

Table 2.10(1)   General Attitude to School (Barker Lunn scales ABCF & G)

	Mixed Ability System	Streamed System
Level of Association		
Gamma	0.096	0.068
Sig of Gamma	NS	NS
Difference between halls in each system		
Chi-Squared	1.103 df=1	0.001 df=1
Sig of Chi-Squared	NS(a)	NS(b)
Difference between systems		
	Chi-Squared=2.659 df=1 NS(c)	

There is no significant association in either system (see Gamma values) and no significant *difference* in the degree of association within the mixed ability system, within the streamed system or between the systems. (See Chi-Squareds a, b and c respectively).

Table 2.10(2)   Attitude to School Class (Barker Lunn scales D & E)

	Mixed Ability System	Streamed System
Level of Association		
Gamma	0.17	0.17
Sig of Gamma	5%	5%
Difference between halls in each system		
Chi-Squared	0.011 df=1	0.057 df=1
Sig of Chi-Squared	NS(a)	NS(b)
Difference between systems		
	Chi-Squared=2.659 df=1 NS(c)	

There is a significant level of association in both systems (see Gamma) but no significant difference in the degree of association within or between the systems (see Chi-Squared values).

Table 2.10(3)   Level of Anxiety/Academic Self Image (Barker Lunn scales HJ)

	Mixed Ability System	Streamed System
Level of Association		
Gamma	—0.120	—0.005
Sig of Gamma	NS	NS
Difference between halls in each system		
Chi-Squared	0.044 df=1	2.68 df=1
Sig of Chi-Squared	NS	NS
Difference between Systems		
	Chi-Squared=0.597 df=1 NS	

There are no significant associations (see Gamma values) nor differences in association within or between the grouping systems, revealed in Table 2.10(3).

Table 2.10(4)   Amount of Social Interaction (ASI scale—1)

	Mixed Ability System	Streamed System
Level of Association		
Gamma	0.010	0.156**
Sig of Gamma	NS	NS
*Difference between halls in each system**		
Chi-Squared	1.70 df=1	see note**
	NS	
Difference between Systems		
	Chi-Squared=3.12 df=1 NS	

**Results have not been included for Drayton

Even though the ASI attitude scale is one administered to the pupils in their fifth year, and therefore represents an up to date assessment of their attitudes, there is still no significant degree of association nor any difference in the level of association within or between grouping systems.

These results indicate that early grouping systems have little influence on the extent to which pupils choose friends of similar attitude. Indeed attitudes, as measured by the Barker Lunn and ASI scales seems to have little to do with friendship formation for only on one scale (Barker Lunn DE) does the level of association reach significance. Were it not for the fact that the ASI results fit into this pattern of low association we might conclude that the year one attitude results were simply an inappropriate measure on which to analyse fourth year friendships. As it is, the ASI results do tend to weaken the force of this criticism. These results should be contrasted with those for first year friendships reported in Phase One (Table 3.68) where it is shown that significant levels of association are reached, in at least one grouping system on nine of the eleven attitude scales.

We might suppose that the increasing maturity of fourth year pupils would widen the basis on which friends are chosen. School itself may well be a less significant part of the lives of many pupils and so attitudes to it may be expected to be of lesser importance in the choice of friends. Without a more extensive programme for testing this remains, of course, nothing more than a plausible hypothesis.

2.4.2.3b **Strong Friends; Analysis by Attitudes**

Since the method of analysis is precisely that used above only a rapid summary of results is given below.

Table 2.11 Association of Strong Friends by Attitude . . . Statistical Summary

Test	MIXED ABILITY SYSTEM			STREAMED SYSTEM			Chi-Squared between Systems
	Gamma	Sig. of Gamma	Fisher between halls (Signif.)	Gamma	Sig. of Gamma	Fisher between halls (Signif.)	
Barker Lunn ABCF & G	0.15	NS	0.637 (NS)	—0.003	NS	0.12 (NS)	0.015 df=1 NS
Barker Lunn D & E	0.21	NS	0.637 (NS)	0.27	5%	0.32 (NS)	0.0003 df=1 NS
Barker Lunn H & J	0.07	NS	0.776 (NS)	0.15	NS	0.12 (NS)	6.547 df=1 5% Greater similarity of HJ score in streamed system

Attitudes ABCFG show no significant association (see Gamma values) and no significant differences in association (see Fisher Test and Chi-Squared values). Attitudes DE reach significant levels of association in the streamed system only. (Gamma=0.27 5%). The differences between the systems and within the mixed ability system are not significant (see Fisher Test and Chi-Squared values).

Attitudes HJ show no significant associations but do show a difference between systems. The streamed system has a greater similarity of HJ scores than the mixed ability system. In Phase One it was discovered that pupils were more likely to choose friends of similar attitude if they were in a mixed ability system. It was suggested that, given a wider spread of people to choose from, pupils were able to make their choice of friends on the basis of attitudes and personalities. The results quoted above offer no evidence that such 'attitude based friendships' are stable, for the degrees of association calculated reach a significant level in only one case and that is in the streamed system.

It is tempting to try to construct hypotheses to explain the levels of association shown above. One could suggest, for example, that the relatively high levels of association on the 'Attitude to School Class' scale in both grouping systems is due to the fact that differences in score on this scale, more perhaps than for either of the other two, are likely to produce behavioural differences in the classroom. Pupils are more likely, therefore, to be aware of one anothers' attitude to class. The slightly greater association in the streamed system is perhaps due to the fact that, in this system, attitude DE scores are highly correlated with VRQ (see Phase One report Table 5.6) and we have already shown that VRQ is itself associated with friendship choice.

A similar sort of explanation can be found for the difference between systems on the HJ scale. There is a negative association between the VRQs of strong friends in the mixed ability system (i.e. people tend to choose as friends those who have different VRQ scores). Phase One showed that, in this system, VRQ was highly correlated with HJ score (see Phase One Table 5.7). One would therefore expect a low degree of association between the HJ scores of strong friends in this system. In the streamed system, however, VRQ of friends is strongly associated and is again positively linked to HJ score (again Table 5.7). We would expect this to lead to the high degree of association between the HJ scores which we have discovered.

2.4.2.4 Analysis by Socio-Economic Group

The Registrar-General's standard scale has been used to classify pupils for this part of the work. The five grades used (we have not divided the middle group into 3 (manual) and 3 (non-manual)) range from professional and executive (1) to basic manual (5). The spread of occupations in Banbury School is shown below :

Table 2.12 Numbers in each category of the Registrar-General's Scale of Socio-Economic Group

Category	1	2	3	4	5
Number	13	70	247	107	7

This rather 'centre heavy' distribution makes it difficult to obtain clear statistical results in this section, nevertheless some results of interest emerge.

Table 2.13 Association by Socio-Economic Group . . . Statistical Summary

Groups	MIXED ABILITY SYSTEM			STREAMED SYSTEM			DIFFERENCES BETWEEN SYSTEMS	
	Gamma	Sig of Gamma	Fisher or (Chi)^2 between Halls (Signif.)	Gamma	Sig of Gamma	Fisher or (Chi)^2 between Halls (Signif.)	(Chi)^2	Significance
All Friends	—0.06	NS	$\chi^2=0.028$ df=1 (NS)	--0.17	NS	$\chi^2=3.12$ df=1 (NS)	0.119 df=1	NS
Strong Friends	—0.486	1%	Fisher=0.60 (NS)	0.182	NS	Fisher=0.20 (NS)	0.039 df=1	NS

It seems that Socio-Economic Group is not an important factor in fourth year choice in either of the grouping systems, and that any differences between systems are small.

In Phase One, it was shown that social class played a more important role in friendship choice in the streamed situation. (See Phase One report Table 3.42). It is clear from the high *negative* association that we find for strong friends in the mixed ability situation, that the 'mixed social class' friendships which were formed in that system *are* long-lasting.

Before placing too much emphasis on this social class result we should perhaps point out that it is what might be expected as a result of the relationship between VRQ and friendship choice; it has been found that VRQ and socio-economic group are significantly correlated ($r=0.25$ significant 1% . . . . result from Phase One).

2.4.2.5 Analysis by Primary School of Origin

Since Primary School of Origin is not a variable which is ordered, use of Gamma to test association is inappropriate. We therefore used the Chi-Squared test alone to compare differences between systems on this criterion. The results are given below :

Table 2.14 Association by Primary School of Origin

	Between Systems		Between Halls Mixed Ability System		Between Halls Streamed System	
	$(Chi)^2$	Signif.	$(Chi)^2$	Signif.	$(Chi)^2$	Signif.
All Friends	0.0026 df=1	NS	5.72 df=1	5%	0.38 df=1	NS
Strong Friends	0.223 df=1	NS	Fisher= 0.016	1%	Fisher= 0.50	NS
			Greater similarity in Wykham in both cases.			

Thus there are no differences between systems, or between halls in the streamed system. The differences for strong friends and all friends in the mixed ability system are both caused by a higher proportion of 'same primary school friendships' in Wykham Hall. A discussion of this result has been given earlier. The fact that the significance of difference between Broughton and Wykham Halls is lower for all friends shows that the influence of primary school on the later formation of friendships is, as one would expect, less powerful.

2.5 Summary

The complete friendship pattern in existence in year four seems to be little affected by the grouping system through which pupils have come. Those who look to mixed ability groupings to provide a greater social homogeneity in schools can however take some comfort from the fact that in the strong friendships, greater mixing by VRQ and socio-economic group does exist amongst pupils whose early grouping background was a mixed ability one. It may well be that a longer exposure to mixed ability groupings would result in a greater proportion of friendships showing this kind of mixing.

Attitude linked friendships were cited in Phase One as evidence that, given a wide spectrum of people from which to choose friends, pupils tended to veer away from ability factors and towards personality ones in deciding their choice. The implication was that these personality based friendships were more natural. There is no evidence here that such friendships survive, or that the habit of forming friends on this criterion is itself firmly enough established to survive the gradual change to more closely streamed groupings. (The only evidence of attitude linkage can, at least in part, be explained in terms of VRQ linkage and the correlation between attitude and VRQ scores). It seems to us doubtful whether any advantage accrues to those pupils who, as a result of their early grouping system, have been able to form friends on personality rather than ability grounds.

An Investigation into Subject Choice

3.1 Introduction

The area of subject choice is both one of national interest and one of particular relevance to the curriculum structure of Banbury School. This happy coincidence has resulted in the expansion of our investigation of this area so that it has come to be a major aspect of the second phase of the project. Under guidance from teachers, form tutors, parents and, no doubt, friends, pupils are asked, during their third year to choose the majority (7 out of 10) of their subjects for year four. Later, at the end of year four they are asked if they would prefer to transfer to Berrymoor for a more vocational fifth year or to continue, in the Upper School, with the programme which they have already chosen for themselves. These are the two points of choice which have come under study. Care has been taken to ensure that the differences found have not been merely the result of teacher popularity and to this end a separate analysis of Drayton School, which operates a very similar option system, has been carried out.

The results are presented in detail below but we give here a brief indication of the trends which have appeared.[1]

   (i)   Differences in subject popularity, as assessed by questionnaire have been discovered. The indications are that Sciences are less popular in the streamed system than they are in the mixed ability system, whereas, for languages, the popularity in the streamed system is greater.
  (ii)   Numbers of pupils finally opting to do particular subjects closely reflect this difference in popularity; the difference in numbers is particularly marked in the case of middle ability girls.
 (iii)   Comparisons between the mean VRQs of those pupils, from each grouping system, who have chosen a particular subject have failed to reveal any significant differences.
  (iv)   The numbers opting for Berrymoor from each grouping background show considerable fluctuation from year to year and do not seem to reflect any trend.
   (v)   The pupils who do opt for Berrymoor seem to come from a narrower (and probably more appropriate) range of ability when their grouping background is streamed.
  (vi)   There seems to be little difference in the extent to which staff prognosis of ability is used in the two grouping systems to guide pupil choice.

3.2 Background Considerations.

The subject choice decision process is passed through by every pupil during the third year. It begins with two separate briefing sessions, one for the pupils and the other for parents, at which details of the system and the sources of help

---

[1] Several studies of subject choice have been made, though little has been done in the context of comprhensive schools. Work to which we have referred is given below :

Bradley J., and Meredith C., "The Relationship of Early Preferences to Sixth Form Specialisation", *J. of Applied Education Studies* 4 (2) 55-6; Hutchings D., *et al*. *"Free to Choose. Origins and Predictions of Academic Specialisation"*, Oxford University Dept. of Educational Studies (1975), Reid M., *et al.*, *"A Matter of Choice—a study of guidance and subject options"*, NFER.

Though the influence of school curriculum structure is often noted explicit study of grouping system effects is rare.

and guidance are explained. Each pupil is then given a copy of the 'Grid' (the pattern of subjects from which he makes his choice) and a set of course descriptions. Copies of the Grids for each group included in this study (Cohort 3 at Banbury School: Streamed in Stanbridge, Mixed Ability in Broughton and Wykham for their first year; Cohort 3 at Drayton: Streamed for their first year, and Cohort 4 at Drayton: Mixed Ability for their first year) are given in Appendix 2. After pupils have been given time to study the Grid offer and make a provisional choice they are interviewed individually by form teachers. The aim of these interviews is to ensure that pupils' programmes are appropriate to their abilities and that the pupils are aware of any limitations on career choice or opportunity for further, or higher, education that might arise as a consequence of the choices made. To help him in this task, the form teacher will have prognosis forms (6-point scale assessments of a pupil's ability) from the individual subject teachers involved with each pupil. He will also call on careers advice and the assistance of the fourth year tutor who is particularly well informed on the requirements of the individual courses. He also has available the files on each pupil, with copies of past reports and of other information. At the time of this personal interview a refinement of the original provisional choice is made. The final stage of consultation is with parents at an evening of individual discussions with form teachers. A high proportion (at least 80%) of parents attend this meeting.

Our study deals mainly with the original un-guided choice made by the pupils. We do not feel that the results would differ greatly if we had, instead, used the final result of the guidance procedure for much guidance is concerned with the level (O-level, CSE or non-exam) at which a subject is studied rather than the actual nature of the subject. At this stage, our work has not differentiated between levels of study. Again, many of our results deal with broad categories of subject (eg. sciences or human studies) and it would be relatively unusual for guidance to deflect a pupil from one such category to another. Nevertheless, by using the original choices we have ensured that our results reflect genuine differences in choice, rather than bias (if any) in the advice given in the two grouping systems.

3.3 Outline of Method

The data used in this chapter has largely been generated by the school in its normal administrative routine. Thus we have made use of the lists of courses opted for by each pupil and the prognosis data which will have been used by form teachers. To this we have added information about subject popularity which was collected by means of a questionnaire issued to all pupils at Banbury and Drayton Schools who fell within Cohort 3. The analyses which follow are based on this data together with background data (VRQ, Socio-Economic Group, Primary School of Origin and Attitude to School) which was available from the work of Phase One.

A matter of particular concern to us was the balance of abilities within the Halls. It is true that Phase One had shown that VRQ and Maths abilities were balanced[1] but it remained possible that pupils in one Hall may be of a higher ability in, for example, spatial reasoning and that this may predispose them towards a study of subjects such as technical drawing where a good three dimensional imagination is of great value. We were able to check this detailed ability background by means of a battery of tests known as the Differential Aptitude Tests.[1] These cover nine separate areas of ability through eight different tests. (Details of the battery are provided in Appendix 5). At this stage it is important to note that

---

[1] For details see Appendix 3.

Bennett G. K., Seashore H. G. and Wiseman A. G., *5th Manual for the Differential Aptitude Tests*, Psychological Corporation, New York.

they are designed to measure aptitude rather than ability so they should provide results which are unaffected by the differences, which may exist in the two grouping systems, in the extent to which the teaching develops pupils' ability in the areas covered by the tests. We should also point out that the battery, while well tested and documented in America, has only just been introduced into this country and the validity in this new cultural environment is still open to debate. Indeed the Grouping Project has the results of these tests available only because Banbury School and Drayton School offered to be pilot schools for the NFER standardisation programme. We are grateful to NFER for permission to include results of this battery in our present work.

After checking the balance of aptitudes within the Halls we studied each subject in turn counting up the number of pupils taking it and the number opting not to take it. We then divided the pupils into ability ranges as described in the chapter on friendship patterns and counted up those pupils in each ability range who had opted for the subject. (In each case the counting process was achieved by means of a computer programme). At various stages in the analysis boys and girls were treated separately.

After this overall check on numbers we measured the mean VRQ, mean attitude score and mean score on each Differential Aptitude Test for the group of pupils from each Hall who had opted for the subject, and compared these means to see of there was any overall difference in the *kind* of pupils from each Hall who had opted for the subject. (In terms of VRQ especially, this comparison proved invaluable in the analysis of public examination results). We then repeated each of these kinds of analysis on subject groups rather than individual subjects, counting up the numbers from each Hall who had, for example, chosen one science, two sciences or three sciences.

Since the constraints on subject choice and the detailed alternatives available were slightly different at Drayton School we carried out all of the above procedures for Drayton as a special case, comparing Drayton Cohort 3 (streamed on entry) with Drayton Cohort 4 (mixed ability on entry). This totally independent check on Banbury School results has enabled us to be fairly certain that we are studying grouping system differences and not simply teacher popularity differences.

We finished our analysis of subject choice by comparing the extent to which the two grouping systems differed in the way in which prognosis information was used to guide choice. This was done by comparing, between systems, the number of subject choices which were sensible in terms of the prognosis, made on the pupil, for that subject, and the number of choices which, on prognosis information alone, could have been replaced by subjects for which the pupil was more suitable.

The choice of Berrymoor was subjected to less detailed analysis, partly because of the smaller numbers involved and the subsequent difficulty of applying statistical procedures to the same sort of sub-groups that we had used for the other work, and partly because Berrymoor as an institution is peculiar to Banbury School so that a detailed study might be of little interest outside the Banbury environment.

3.4 Statement of Results

3.4.1 The overall balance of aptitude within the Halls

The analysis of this balance was based on the Differential Aptitude Test battery as we felt that a more detailed analysis of the comparability of the samples in the two systems was required, than could be provided by a study of VRQ alone.

The areas of ability tested by the Differential Aptitude Test battery are listed in the table below :

24

Table 3.1 Tests comprising the Differential Aptitude Test Battery

Test Name	Symbol	Brief Description of Aptitude under Test
Verbal Reasoning	VR	How clearly does one think and reason with words?
Numerical Ability	NA	How clearly does one think and reason with numbers?
Combined Result VR+NA	VN	General Scholastic Aptitude.
Abstract Reasoning	AR	Can one handle ideas not presented in words and numbers?
Space Relations	SR	Can one think 'in three dimensions'?
Mechanical Reasoning	MR	Can one think clearly about simple machines?
Clerical Speed/Accuracy	CS	Can one process simple tasks quickly and accurately?
Spelling	SP	How accurately can one spell?
Language Usage	LU	How well can one recognise errors in grammar, punctuation and sentence construction?

Drayton and Banbury Schools were dealt with separately in the analysis. For Banbury School, the mean score for the pupils in Cohort 3 in each Hall was computed. These means, and the corresponding standard deviations were compared using the F ratio test to compare the standard deviations and the t test to compare the means. (For comment on the meaning of the F and t tests, and their inter-relationship, the reader is referred to Chapter 8.) For Drayton School, the means and standard deviations for the pupils in Cohorts 3 and 4 were computed and these results compared using the same statistical techniques. The results are presented below.

Table 3.2 BANBURY SCHOOL Cohort 3 Values of Mean Dif.Ap. scores.

Hall	Statistic	VR	NA	VN	AR	CS	MR	SR	SP	LU
Broughton	Mean	22.49	14.03	36.43	32.66	38.05	37.75	30.04	58.67	27.33
	Standard Deviation	10.84	8.33	17.94	9.90	11.23	13.38	10.86	18.25	9.85
	No.	102	101	101	98	103	103	103	103	103
Wykham	Mean	23.11	13.11	36.22	32.62	46.29	41.01	29.08	44.95	27.18
	Standard Deviation	11.26	6.94	16.50	10.17	13.49	9.68	11.96	18.42	10.33
	No.	114	114	114	109	109	109	109	110	109
Stanbridge	Mean	22.92	13.03	35.95	31.40	38.85	53.57	28.25	57.10	27.21
	Standard Deviation	11.26	7.48	17.25	11.12	12.68	10.60	12.40	17.95	10.47
	No.	97	97	97	97	97	97	97	97	97

Table 3.3 BANBURY SCHOOL Cohort 3 Hall by Hall Comparison of Mean Dif.Ap. Results

Halls	Deg. of Freedom	VR	NA	VN	AR	CS	MR	SR	SP	LU
Br v Wy										
F test	101,113	1.08	1.44	1.18	1.05	1.44	1.91*	1.21	1.02	1.10
t test	215	0.06	0.13	0.00	0.00	0.38	0.22	0.06	0.31	0.00
Br v St										
F test	101,96	1.08	1.24	1.08	1.26	1.27	1.60	1.30	1.03	1.13
t test	198	0.00	0.11	0.02	0.06	0.00	0.77	0.10	0.02	0.00
Wy v St										
F test	113,96	1.00	1.16	1.09	1.20	1.13	1.20	1.08	1.05	1.03
t test	210	0.06	0.00	0.03	0.06	0.34	0.85	0.05	0.28	0.00

* F is significant at 5% (variance in Br is higher.)

Since three Halls are compared against one another, there are three comparisons rather than one for each Differential Aptitude scale in this table. There is therefore three times the chance that statistically significant results may rise spuriously. To guard against the possibility of undue importance being attached to such results it is usual to carry out an analysis of variance and then, if necessary F and t tests. This would indeed have been a *required* procedure if the F and t tests which are reported in Table 3.3 had shown several significances. As we have shown only one significance, the logic of the F and t tests alone is sound, and the omission of the usual analysis of variance is not a matter of great importance.

Table 3.4 DRAYTON SCHOOL Cohorts 3 and 4 Mean Dif.Ap. Scores

Cohort	Statistic	VR	NA	VN	AR	CS	MR	SR	SP	LU
C3 Streamed	Mean	23.95	13.16	37.11	31.99	42.29	42.42	29.26	59.98	26.87
	Standard Deviation	9.65	6.31	14.38	9.30	10.65	10.10	10.20	17.24	9.03
	Number	131	131	131	130	131	131	131	131	131
C4 Mixed Ability	Mean	21.18	10.88	32.08	28.94	40.22	39.66	24.73	55.13	23.15
	Standard Deviation	8.72	5.04	12.23	11.53	10.52	9.94	8.89	14.48	9.20
	Number	136	136	136	138	138	138	138	138	138

Table 3.5 DRAYTON SCHOOL Comparison of C3 and C4 means

Comparison Group	Degrees of Freedom	VR	NA	VN	AR	CS	MR	SR	SP	LU
Drayton C3/ Drayton C4										
F test	137,130	1.22	1.56	1.38	1.51	1.02	1.03	1.32	1.41	1.03
t test	268	2.44*	3.25**	3.07**	2.37*	1.60	2.29*	3.87***	2.49*	3.34**

Notes : (1) *   means that the difference is significant at 5%
      (2) **   means that the difference is significant at 1%
      (3) *** means that the difference is significant at 0.1%
      (4) F or t without a quoted level of significance are not significantly different.

It is immediately apparent that the Banbury School Halls are very closely matched (no significant differences on t test and only one on F test) whereas the two consecutive intakes at Drayton are significantly different on all aptitudes except Clerical Speed and Accuracy.

The implications of Banbury School results are simple. Differences found between the numbers of pupils from each Hall who chose a particular subject, cannot be attributed to the chance allocation, to one or more Halls, of pupils with those aptitudes (as measured by Differential Aptitude Tests) which are probably relevant to that subject. The difference must be a difference in choice and not a difference in aptitude. It is possible that one or more Halls may teach in such a way as to more effectively convert the aptitudes which we have measured into abilities, and that the difference in choice is the result of the development of greater specialist ability for a subject in this/these Hall(s). At this stage it is not possible to distinguish between the 'difference in developed ability' hypothesis and the 'simple difference in choice' hypothesis. With the help in the work of the chapter reporting on the performance of pupils in public exams, it may be possible to choose between these alternative explanations of the differences set out below.

The situation in Drayton is rather more complicated. Table 3.4 shows that the means do differ considerably and Table 3.5 confirms that these differences are significant (eg. likely to occur by chance less than 5 times in 100 where the significance level of the result is stated as 5%). It should be noted that in all aptitudes, Cohort 3 has a higher score than Cohort 4. (This is even true of Clerical Speed and Accuracy where the differences fail to reach significant levels). To help in the interpretation of the scores it is useful to know whether C3 is un-usually high or C4 unusually low. We decided between these alternatives by comparing C3 at Drayton with C3 at Banbury School.

Table 3.6 Cohort 3 Drayton/Banbury comparison

Comparison Group	Degrees of Freedom	VR	NA	VN	AR	CS	MR	SR	SP	LU
Br v Dr										
F test	101,130	1.26	1.74*	1.56	1.13	1.11	1.68*	1.13	1.12	1.19
t test	232	0.07	0.14	0.03	0.08	0.25	0.27	0.07	0.02	0.09
Wy v Dr										
F test	113,130	1.36	1.21	1.32	1.19	1.60	1.13	1.38	1.14	1.31
t test	244	0.00	0.00	0.03	0.08	0.21	0.08	0.00	0.37	0.08
St v Dr										
F test	96,130	1.36	1.41	1.44	1.43	1.42	1.06	1.48	1.08	1.34
t test	227	0.07	0.00	0.06	0.00	0.22	0.75	0.06	0.05	0.88

* shows that the variances differ by an amount which is significant at the 5% level.

We see from Table 3.6 that Drayton Cohort 3 is closely comparable to the Ban-bury School Cohort 3. It is reasonable to suggest that Drayton Cohort 4, then, is lower in its Differential Aptitude Test results. The overall lowering is almost certainly due to the fact Cohort 4 was one year younger when tested than Cohort 3.[1]

However, in relation to the present work it is important to note than C4 pupils are *particularly* low compared with C3 pupils in the areas of Numerical Ability (t test significance=1%) Space Relations (t test significance=0.1%) and Lang-uage Usage (t test significance=1%). We would therefore be surprised if C4 pupils, when compared with C3 pupils, made a greater number of choices of, for example, physical sciences (where one might suppose that a higher aptitude in the areas quoted would lead to greater enjoyment of and success in these subjects and therefore predispose pupils towards the choice of them).

Since some of the final analyses of subject choice involve the study of boys and girls separately we conclude this study of the comparability of samples by com-paring boys' and girls' scores on each of the Differential Aptitude Tests. Table 3.7 gives the mean and standard deviation results for Banbury School boys and girls separately, and Table 3.8 gives the results of statistical comparisons between these means.

Table 3.7 Cohort 3 Banbury School Sex differences.

Comparison Group	Statistic	VR	NA	VN	AR	CS	MR	SR	SP	LU
Boys	Mean	23.66	13.96	37.58	32.78	38.78	45.60	31.73	53.71	25.80
	Standard Deviation	10.59	7.45	16.52	10.35	11.38	10.14	11.78	18.12	9.56
	Number	149	149	149	149	149	149	149	149	149
Girls	Mean	22.95	12.75	35.75	32.07	42.44	37.85	26.48	57.21	28.71
	Standard Deviation	10.47	6.77	15.68	9.63	12.11	8.39	10.00	18.93	9.84
	Number	164	164	164	164	164	164	164	164	164

[1] See Bennett G. K., Seashore H. G., and Wiseman A. G., *op cit* where in Chapter 3, norms for different age groups are presented.

Table 3.8 Comparison of Mean Scores of Boys and Girls C3 Banbury School.

Comparison Group	Degrees of Freedom	VR	NA	VN	AR	CS	MR	SR	SP	LU
Boys v. Girls										
F test	148,163	1.02	1.21	1.11	1.16	1.14	1.46	1.39	1.09	1.06
t test	312	0.60	1.50	1.01	0.17	2.76**	6.75***	4.22***	1.74	2.63*

     *   significant at 5%
     ** significant at 1%
     *** significant at 0.1%

Tables 3.7 and 3.8 together tell us that the boys in the sample have higher aptitude for Mechnical Reasoning and Space Relations and the girls, higher aptitude for Clerical Speed and Accuracy and Language Usage.

Other studies have revealed similar sex differences in spatial ability. Droege[1] (1967) and Flanagan et al[2] (1961) have shown in America, that boys' scores exceeded girls' "by at least 0.40 standard score units by the end of high school". A study on 102 14-year olds by Nash[3] (1973) using Differential Aptitude Tests and Group Administered Embedded Figure Tests also showed higher scores for boys. A general review of this and other sex differences can be found in *The Psychology of Sex Differences* by Maccoby, E. E., and Jacklin, C. N. (Oxford University Press 1975).

3.4.2 Subject Popularity.

An early indication of pupils' attitudes towards individual subjects was obtained by asking all Cohort 3 pupils at Banbury and Drayton Schools to list, in order of preference, the subjects which they had studied in their third year. A full list of subjects taught in year three was appended to the questionnaire so that there was no risk of subjects being omitted unintentionally. The questionnaire was quite specific in asking for the pupil's own personal preference, independent of his ability in the subject and his own awareness of the importance usually attached to the subject.

In analysing the results of this questionnaire we made use of the top two choices made by each pupil. We totalled, for each hall separately, the number of times each subject appeared amongst these top two choices and then combined subjects together into groups to produce the following table.

Table 3.9 Number of 'top two choices' for each subject in each Hall

Hall	Sub.Area	Sci	Hum St.	Maths	Eng	Lang	PE	Design	Music	Totals
Stanbridge		25	52	12	26	13	19	37	1	203
Drayton		40	61	17	20	23	39	75	8	283
Broughton		55	51	20	11	7	15	15	9	185
Wykham		53	31	17	19	3	32	55	3	248

The exact composition of each subject area is given in Appendix 7.

---

[1] Droege, R. C., "Sex Differences in Aptitude Maturation During High School". *J. Counselling Psychology 1967, 14, 407-11.*

[2] Flanagan, J. C., *et al. Counsellors Technical Manual for Interpreting Test Scores (Project Talent)* Palo Alto California 1961.

[3] Nash, S. C., *Conceptions and Concomitants of Sex Role Stereotyping.* Doctoral Thesis (unpublished) Columbia University 1973.

Each subject group was then analysed to compare the frequency of choice.
  (i)   between the streaming and mixed ability systems (ie St&Dr v Br&W)
  (ii) between the Halls in the streamed system (ie St v Dr)
  (iii) between the Halls in the mixed ability system (ie Br v Wy)
One such analysis is set out in full below.

Table 3.10 Analysis within and between systems of the popularity of the Science subject group.

Hall or System	No. Choosing	No. not Choosing	Total	Chi-Squared	df	Significance
BETWEEN SYSTEMS						
Br + Wy (M.A.)	108	325	433	19.30	1	0.1%
St + Dr (Str)	65	421	486			
WITHIN STREAMED SYSTEM						
Stanbridge	25	178	203	0.20	1	NS
Drayton	40	243	283			
WITHIN MIXED ABILITY						
Broughton	55	130	185	3.52	1	NS
Wykham	53	195	248			

Thus we have a highly significant difference between the two grouping systems with science being far more popular in the mixed ability system. Between the individual halls in each system the differences are not significant.

An identical study was made of the other subject areas. Table 3.11 shows a summary of the results of the Chi-Squared tests. (These can all be computed from Table 3.9).

Table 3.11 Statistical Summary of all subject groups.

Subject Group	Between Systems			Within Streaming			Within Mixed Ability		
	Chi^2	df	Signif.	Chi^2	df	Signif.	Chi^2	df	Signif.
Science	19.3(M)	1	0.1%	0.20(–)	1	NS	3.52(–)	1	NS
Human Studies	2.29(–)	1	NS	0.87(–)	1	NS	14.70(B)	1	0.1%
Maths	1.91(–)	1	NS	0.02(–)	1	NS	1.64(–)	1	NS
English	1.63(–)	1	NS	3.90(St)	1	5%	0.25(–)	1	NS
Languages	11.46(S)	1	0.1%	0.29(–)	1	NS	0.25(–)	1	NS
P.E.	0.21(–)	1	NS	1.79(–)	1	NS	0.00(–)	1	NS
Design	2.62(–)	1	NS	4.12(D)	1	5%	4.72(W)	1	5%
Music	0.50(–)	1	NS	numbers too small			numbers too small		

(M)=higher popularity in mixed ability system
(S) = higher popularity in streamed system
(St)=higher popularity in Stanbridge
(D) =higher popularity in Drayton
(W)=higher popularity in Wykham
(B) = higher popularity in Broughton

These tables show clear differences between the two grouping systems in the extent to which sciences and languages are popular in those systems. But, in these subject areas, they show *no* difference between the two communities which make up each system. The second point makes it possible to put in doubt the simple idea that this difference in popularity of subject is merely the result of teacher popularity differences. We should remember that by the time the students filled in the questionnaire, they may well have met as many as seven science teachers and that many science teachers teach in halls in both systems. In view of this, it is not likely that streamed classes were taught by unpopular teachers and mixed ability classes by popular ones to such a degree that a 0.1% level of significance could be achieved in the difference in subject popularity. Similar considerations apply to the difference in popularity of languages.

An alternative explanation for the differences in sciences rests on the fact that the facilities available must play an important part in the enjoyment to be gained by pupils from the study of science. It should be remembered however that all Banbury School third year pupils do their science in the same laboratories in the middle school science block. There may, however, have been some carry over from the laboratory situation that they met in their first and second year which may contribute to the difference. When one turns to languages, there is no 'environmental explanation' which can be called up on the explain the differences. We are led to speculate on whether the style of teaching which is possible in a particular grouping system might favour the good presentation of some subjects but hinder that of others. Detailed observation of teaching style were beyond the manpower resources of the project and it remains an interesting and indeed tantalising speculation.

Tables 3.10 and 3.11 also show some important differences *within* each grouping system between the popularity in the two halls, of Design, English and Human Studies. With the aruguments from the previous paragraph in mind it is perhaps interesting to note that design classes were taught predominantly within their own hall by hall based staff, so that teacher and facilities might more easily be the cause of the difference, and that English teaching too is done predominantly by hall-based staff. In any case some differences between individual halls (whether they operate the same grouping system or not) are to be expected simply as a consequence of the halls' individual characteristics. We feel that where the 'within system' differences were small, but the 'between system' differences were large (eg. in sciences and languages) there was a strong indication (though not a definite proof) that it was the grouping system which had influenced the result. We should also note that, over more than twenty tests, some 5% significances might well be due simply to chance.

It should perhaps be pointed out that, for clarity, Drayton School has been referred to above as if it were still a hall of Banbury School.

3.4.3 Subject Choice—The Numbers of Pupils Choosing Particular Subjects

Section 3.4.2 shows some differences between grouping systems in the kinds of subject which are popular amongst pupils. It is the aim of this section to determine whether or not this difference in popularity is reflected in a difference in the numbers of pupils from each system who actually choose to study particular subjects in the fourth year.[1]

In relating the results found in Section 3.4.2 to those of this section is is important to remember the constraints on subject choice which are imposed on the pupils by the system. These are stated in full in Appendix 2 but the main features are repeated here for the convenience of the reader.

All pupils have to study Maths and English together with a core of short courses which alternate with one another throughout the year. These include Health Education (as distinct from Health Science—which is a science department course mainly for lower ability girls) Careers, P.E. (which interested pupils can augment by further choice of PE as one of their options), R.E. (which can also be chosen as a specialist option), Library and Music (which, like PE and RE can be augmented by specialist study). All pupils must choose one science subject, one Human Study (see Appendix 7), and one subject from the Design/Music/PE subject group.

In addition to these basic constraints pupils have to satisfy their form teacher that their options are sensible in relation to their abilities. Pupils may also be constrained by the fact that two subjects which they would like to choose fall

---

[1] Strong links between 3rd year subject preference and *6th* form subject choice have been disclosed by Bradley & Meredith in *J. of Applied Educational Studies* 4(2), pp. 55-57.

in the same grid block and are not repeated elsewhere in the grid. In such a case one subject would have to be dropped. The design of the grid is such that cases of this kind are rare.

It is perhaps worth noting that the time spent on each subject, including Maths and English, is identical.

The tables in Appendix 6 present the basic data for this part of the study. They give the numbers of pupils in each hall, and in each of Cohorts 3 and 4 at Drayton School, who choose each individual subject. Also shown are the numbers choosing *at least* one subject from each subject area and the numbers choosing one, two and three subjects from each subject area.

Some of this data is shown sub-divided by VRQ and by sex.

3.4.3.1 Subject Group Comparisons.

The tables which follow present the main results which were obtained from these basic figures by use of Chi-Squared and Fisher Exact Probability tests.

Table 3.12 Comparison of numbers choosing one, two and three subjects from each subject area.

SUBJECT AREA	No. Choosing a	No. Not Choosing a	Between Halls (Chi)^2 b	Signif. c	Between Systems (Chi)^2 d	Signif. e	Within Mix. Ab.Sys. (Chi)^2 f	Signif. g
SCIENCES								
One Science only	B 20	51						
	W 22	73	9.2	1%	7.97	1%	0.3	NS
	S 36	46						
	D3 75	66			6.1	1%		
	D4 52	86						
Two Sciences	B 35	36						
	W 52	43	3.7	NS	2.78	NS	0.29	NS
	S 33	49						
	D3 40	101			8.91	1%		
	D4 64	74						
Three Sciences	B 16	55						
	W 21	74	1.4	NS	1.04	NS	0.01	NS
	S 13	69						
	D3 22	119			0.005	NS		
	D4 21	117						
LANGUAGES No language	B 36	35						
	W 39	56	4.9	10%[1]	2.92	10%[1]	1.16	NS
	S 27	55						
	D3 39	102			4.11	5%		
	D4 55	83						
One language	B 22	49						
	W 37	58	3.2	NS	1.74	NS	0.80	NS
	S 37	45						
	D3 69	72			0.003	NS		
	D4 67	71						

[1] The 10% signfiances quoted above should be treated with caution. They are quite likely to arise by chance in such a large number of tests. They are included simply to draw the reader's attention to the trends displayed by the corresponding figures.

31

Table 3.12 continued.

SUBJECT AREA		No. Choosing a	No. Not Choosing a	Between Halls (Chi)² b	Signif. c	Between Systems (Chi)² d	Signif. e	Within Mix.Ab.Sys. (Chi)² f	Signif. g
Two languages	B	13	58						
	W	19	76	0.3	NS	0.1	NS	0.06	NS
	S	12	64						
	D3	33	108						
	D4	16	122						
HUMAN STUDIES									
One Human Study Only	B	38	33						
	W	44	51	6.03	5%	4.57	5%	0.58	NS
	S	28	54						
	D3	37	104			6.4	5%		
	D4	57	81						
Two Human Studies	B	31	40						
	W	45	50	7.06	5%	6.14	5%	0.10	NS
	S	52	30						
	D3	76	65			0.19	NS		
	D4	79	59						
Three Human Studies	B	2	69						
	W	4	91	Numbers too small for chi² analysis[1]					
	S	2	80						
	D3	25	116	Numbers too small for chi² analysis[1]					
	D4	1	137						
DESIGN									
One Design Only	B	25	46						
	W	44	51	2.65	NS	0.37	NS	1.63	NS
	S	30	52						
	D3	40	101			0.01	NS		
	D4	41	97						
Two or more Design Subjects	B	35	36						
	W	46	49	0.14	NS	0.05	NS	0.002	NS
	S	42	40						
	D3	82	59			0.07	NS		
	D4	77	61						

[1] Analysis of difference in proportion shows that the difference between D3 and D4 is significant at 0.1%. The difference between grouping systems at Banbury School is not significant.

Table 3.12 contains some important results. Columns 'a' give the number of pupils (both boys and girls, all VRQ ranges) who choose to do, for example, only one science. In columns 'b' and 'c' the separate halls are compared using the Chi-Squared test to see if the difference in numbers are statistically significant. Column 'c' gives the level of significance expressed as a percentage. An entry of 1% in this column means that there is less than a 1% likelihood of such a magnitude of difference arising merely by chance. The letters NS in this column imply that the difference is not significant (ie. quite likely to arise merely by chance). Columns 'b' and 'c' are also used to compare the two cohort C3 (streamed on entry) and C4 (mixed ability on entry) at Drayton School. Columns 'd' to 'g' are used for Banbury School only. Columns 'd' and 'e' give the significance of difference between the systems. This result is derived by comparing Broughton and Wykham Halls taken together, with Stanbridge Hall alone. Columns 'f' and 'g' compare the difference between Broughton and Wykham and therefore test the significance of any difference between the halls which make up the mixed ability system.

If we turn first to the results for the science subject area we see that 42 pupils out of 166 in the mixed ability system choose to do only one science and that the same decision is made by 36 pupils out of 82 in the streamed system. Thus a higher proportion of 'Streamed pupils' opt for only one science. We see from columns 'b' and 'c' that this difference in numbers is highly significant (Chi-Squared$=7.97$ . . . 1%). Since all pupils must choose at least one science this result represents a move away from science on the part of 'Streamed pupils'.

An over-riding confirmation of the dependence of the numbers choosing on the grouping system comes from the Drayton School result. Here in C3, 75 out of 141 streamed pupils' choose only one science, whereas in C4 52 out of 138 'mixed ability pupils' choose only one science. Again far more streamed pupils are in effect opting away from sciences and again the statistics confirm that the size of the difference is such as to occur less than one time in a hundred by mere chance. The only thing that the two sets of pupils (Banbury School, Broughton and Wykham and Drayton Cohort 4) have in common is their mixed ability background and the suggestion is quite clear that this background has to some extent influenced the choice of science.

The Drayton result is rather unexpected as Drayton C4 had particularly low Differential Aptitude scores on those aptitudes which we would expect to lead one towards a liking of science. It is perhaps worth noting that the chance of both of these results at Drayton and Banbury schools occurring together simply by chance, is very small indeed since they are independent results each occurring less than once in a hundred times from chance alone.

In Drayton the difference between the two systems in the choice of two sciences is also highly significant but this time with the proportions the other way round. We have then a far higher choice of two sciences on the part of the mixed ability cohort. At Banbury School the picture is not quite so clear but even here we see that the proportions choosing two and three sciences from the mixed ability halls were both higher than the proportion choosing from the streamed hall. (In this case however neither of these differences reached the levels required for statistical significance.)

We can summarise the results on the choice of science as follows :

Drayton School Mixed Ability Cohort tends to choose two sciences Streamed Cohort tends to choose one science only.

Banbury School Mixed Ability Halls tend to choose two or three sciences. Streamed Hall tends to choose only one science.

This can be seen to be in complete accord with the subject popularity result.

Similar results can be seen in the languages and human studies subject areas. Again their is no significant difference within the mixed ability system at Banbury School, and good agreement between the Banbury and Drayton results in terms of both direction and magnitude of any differences. We find that for languages there is a higher level of participation in the streamed situation (the clearest indication coming from the results for no choice of a language), and that for human studies, there is also greater participation in the streamed situation. It should however be remembered that pupils must choose seven subjects and that a tendency to choose one rather than two sciences may well force a reciprocal tendency in another subject area.

33

Before moving on to consider individual subjects we would like to point out one more implication of the figures in table 3.12. Although the differences in the mixed ability system never reach a high enough level to be significant, they do lend considerable support to the idea that the differences discussed above really do come about as a result of grouping system differences. This support arises because Wykham persevered with mixed ability groupings for most subjects in year two whereas Broughton was streamed in year two for everything except French, History, Geography, RE, PE, Music and Design.

Thus Broughton was streamed for year two science and this is reflected in a higher proportion in Broughton than in Wykham choosing only one science (20/71 in Broughton compared with only 22/95 in Wykham). This is in the right direction to support the idea that streaming deflects pupils from science choice.

3.4.3.2 Individual Subject Comparisons

If the subject group results arise because of teacher preference, differences must exist in individual subjects which make up the group as well as in the overall subject group figures. We have therefore studied individual subjects separately taking the basic data from the tables in Appendix 6.

We give below all the results of this study which reached statistical significance.

Table 3.13 Statistically signficant differences . . . Individual Subjects

SUBJECT	CHI-SQUARED	SIG. LEVEL	HALLS SHOWING HIGH OR LOW NUMBERS OF CHOOSERS	
BANBURY				
Business St.	9.65	1%	S high	W low
Draw & Paint	6.42	5%	W high	B low
Tech./Elect.	14.19	0.5%	B high	S low
Computer St.	7.00	5%	W high	S low
PE	9.05	2.5%	W high	S low
Dance	6.84	5%	W high	B low
French	7.42	2.5%	S high	B low
RE	7.96	2.5%	W high	S low
DRAYTON				
Chemistry	8.86	1%	C4 high	
Art	4.13	5%	C3 high	
French	6.88	1%	C3 high	
RE	8.41	1%	C3 high	
Cultural St.	33.31	0.1%	C3 high	

Since some 80 subjects at Banbury and Drayton schools were studied, some 5% and 2.5% signifiances would be expected to arise purely by chance. When this and the nature of the subjects quoted above are borne in mind there can be little support here for the teacher preference hypothesis. Where individual subjects are considered the direction of the differences does support the subject group picture (eg. French: Stanbridge high numbers; Broughton low). This is even so of those subjects for which the differences are not significant (see, for example, Physics in Table A6.1).

3.4.3.3 Analysis of Subject Group Choice in relation to VRQ.

(i) This section attempts to examine whether the differences so far reported are spread across the whole VRQ range or whether they are specific to one particular ability level. The VRQ values used in this work were measured at the end of the pupils' first year. These were the most up-to-date results available to us. Where, as a result of absence from school etc, the pupils' result at the end of year one was not available, we were forced to use that measured at the beginning of year one. The number of times this occurred was small.

The VRQ values, which was chosen to define the three ranges that we used, (high, medium and low ability), were such as to produce groups of pupils who were recognisable as weak, moderate or bright pupils. To this end we tried to make the VRQ divisions match the streaming divisions which were already well understood within the school. We felt that this would also be widely accepted outside, as producing a meaningful division of the sample into subgroups which were genuinely different in terms of academic prowess. Thus the divisions were chosen so as to put roughly 20% of the sample into the low VRQ range, 60% into the medium range and the remaining 20% into the high VRQ range. The low range consists therefore of predominantly non-exam pupils, the high range, of O-level 'grammar school type' pupils and the middle range, of CSE and weak O-level pupils.

The actual VRQ values used to define these ranges were as shown in Table 3.14.

Table 3.14   VRQ Ranges

Range	VRQ score
Low	85 and below
Medium	86—109
High	110 and above

The *mean* VRQ score obtained in the "end of year one assessment" was 100.8.

The analysis of the kind shown in Table 3.12 was repeated for each of these VRQ ranges separately. No significant differences of any kind were found in the low VRQ range. (Raw data in Tables A6.3 and A6.7). The results for the middle VRQ range are shown below.

Table 3.15   Subject Group Analysis . . . Mid VRQ Range Only

Comparison Group		Chi-Squared	Signif. Level	Hall or Cohort with a Large Number Choosing
B+W:S	1 Sci	5.09	5%	S
	2 Sci	6.57	5%	B+W
	3 Sci	0.12	NS	—
D3 : D4	1 Sci	10.7	1%	D3
	2 Sci	10.0	1%	D4
	3 Sci	0.01	NS	—
B+W : S	No Lang.	5.14	5%	B+W
	1 Lang.	4.32	5%	S
	2 Lang.	0.00	NS	—
D3 : D4	No Lang.	4.74	5%	D4
	1 Lang.	4.24	5%	D3
	2 Lang.	0.02	NS	—
B+W : S	1 Hum St.	3.21	10%	B+W
	2 Hum St.	4.55	5%	S
D3 : D4	1 Hum St.	3.03	10%	D4
	2 Hum St.	1.05	NS	—
B+W : S	1 Design	0.01	NS	—
	2 Design or more	0.03	NS	—
D3 : D4	1 Design	0.31	NS	—
	2 Design or more	2.27	NS	—

We find, in this medium ability range, all of the effects reported earlier. It is particularly interesting that even at this more detailed level Drayton and Banbury

Schools remain similar. The fact that the common feature is the grouping system cannot be too strongly emphaised.

In the high VRQ range only two significant differences show up, both of them at Drayton School. They show Cohort 3 opting for two languages more than Cohort 4 (significance level 2%) and Cohort 4 opting for one language more than Cohort 3 (significance level 1%). These results are in the same direction as the overall results already reported.

Apart from this one high VRQ result we are led to believe that all of the differences reported and discussed in Section 3.4.3.1 are differences which occur in the middle VRQ range, ie. predominantly between CSE pupils.

(ii) An alternative method of studying the relationship between VRQ and subject choice was undertaken in an attempt to shed some light on the suggestion that counselling in the streamed system was more "VRQ-conscious". This suggestion arises from the fact that pupils in a streamed system are labelled (by the stream to which they are allocated) according to their VRQ. It is possible, therefore, that guidance on subject choice could be influenced by this *label* as much as, or perhaps even more than, by a pupil's individual strengths and weaknesses. Such a dependence on VRQ labels might imply that there would be a strong tendency to guide high VRQ pupils towards the subjects traditionally thought of as "hard" and the low VRQ pupils towards the "softer options" irrespective of the pupils' individual aptitudes in the areas which are especially relevant to those subjects. We would expect an effort of this kind to show up if a comparison is made of the range of VRQ scores found for the pupils from each grouping system who choose each subject. If counselling is more VRQ-conscious in the streamed system we would expect a smaller range of VRQ for streamed pupils choosing the "hard" and "soft" subjects.

Although F test comparisons between Broughton plus Wykham and Stanbridge students and between Drayton Cohort 3 and Drayton Cohort 4 were made for all subjects, no significant differences in the range of VRQ scores were detected. Similar comparisons were done for those choosing one, two and three subjects within each subject group. Three science and two language choices are traditionally "hard options" and several design choices is very much thought of as a "soft option". Nevertheless, even here, no significant differences in the range of VRQ scores were detected. What is more, there was even no consistent *trend* towards smaller spreads of VRQ for streamed pupils. We feel that there is no evidence in this work to suggest that labelling through streaming influences guidance on subject choice.

3.4.3.4 Analysis of Subject Group Choice in relation to sex.

When the choice patterns of boys and girls are looked at separately very few differences between halls or grouping systems appear for the boys. Indeed, for them, the only difference which reached a 5% level of significance was on two language choice at Drayton School where there was more choice of two languages from the streamed cohort. (Chi-squared between streamed and mixed ability cohorts=5.15 df=1 significance=5%).

The results for the girls alone are more complex and are quoted in full below.

Table 3.16 Subject Group Comparisons. Girls Only.

Comparison Group		Chi-Squared	Signif. Level	Hall or Cohort with a Large number choosing
B+W : S	1 Sci	8.73	1%	S
	2 Sci	4.13	5%	B+W
D3 : D4	1 Sci	7.32	1%	D3
	2 Sci	9.49	1%	D4

B+W :S	No Lang.	4.03	5%	B+W
B+W :S	2 Hum St.	4.99	5%	B
D3 : D4	1 Hum St.	4.51	5%	D4

No other differences are significant at 5% level.

Thus we can further reduce the subgroup responsible for the differences reported in 3.4.3.1 it appears that the differences are due predominantly to the middle ability girls.

An interesting possible explanation of these differences now presents itself. We saw in Tables 3.7 and 3.8 that girls are less successful on Differential Aptitude tests of Mechanical Reasoning and Space Relations than boys. These are the kinds of aptitude which would lead to success in science and the lower scores may well explain why girls in a streamed group (where they are, overall, of equal ability to the boys but where they may well be less capable in these areas) feel themselves to be inferior to the boys, and therefore opt away from science choices. The middle ability girls in a mixed ability group will of course find themselves to be of higher ability, even in these specific areas, than *some* of the boys in that group, and may well therefore increase in confidence and ultimately choose a science course in year four.

3.5 Choice of Berrymoor.

With the raising of the school leaving age, considerations of space forced Banbury School to seek ways of accommodating some 125 fifth year pupils who could not be fitted into the existing Upper School buildings. This challenge was seen also as an opportunity to provide the best possible curriculum for the new fifth former. Through linked timetabling, the school already had close contacts with the local technical college and, prior to RoSLA many 15 and 16 year olds had made use of its facilities to follow predominatly vocational courses. The decision was made to solve the problem of accommodation, and the curriculum problem by establishing a satellite unit of the Upper School in temporary classrooms near the technical college site, and through this unit, which became known as the Berrymoor Unit, to build on the already established demand for vocational education by providing an integrated course of 'academic' core subjects (Maths, English, History and Geography) and vocational options (such as Engineering, Construction, Agriculture, Catering, Secretarial, Fashion courses). The core subjects are taught by school staff permanently based in the unit and the option courses are staffed by the technical college.

Pupils opt for the unit during their fourth year. Counselling is intended to deflect from the unit, the very able and the least able pupils who, it is felt, are better served in the main Upper School. In all the work which follows we have used data for those pupils who have actually been accepted for the unit so the result reflect a combination of differences in pupil choice and differences in counselling.

Drayton School pupils (and indeed others from schools near Banbury) are able to attend the unit but entry policy (which gives Drayton a quota roughly equivalent to one Hall of Banbury School despite its much bigger size) makes it difficut to include Drayton in the analysis. We have often, therefore, omitted Drayton from our results. There is no quota system for the individual Halls of Banbury School so it remains possible to compare the tendancy for pupils from different halls to choose to attend the unit.

Since Berrymoor is an unusual, if not unique, development, detailed results on, for example course choice, would be of limited interest outside the Banbury situation. This, together with the fact that the sample is fairly small so that numbers in subgroups within it are always small, has encouraged us to present

37

only a very general analysis of the way in which the halls differ in the extent to which their pupils choose to attend the unit.

3.5.1 Background Data—Aptitudes of Pupils Opting for Berrymoor

Our first aim is to indicate the overall quality of the pupils who have opted for Berrymoor. We therefore give below the mean differential aptitude scores for those pupils, together with the mean scores for their colleagues in Cohort 3 who opted instead to move into the Upper School. In order that one might assess the importance of the differences which are apparent, we ran F ratio and t tests and give that information also in the table.

Table 3.17   Mean Differential Aptitude scores at Berrymoor and Upper School Cohort 3

Statistic	VR	NA	VN	AR	CS	MR	SR	SP	LU
Berrymoor									
Mean	16.28	9.40	25.73	27.63	35.64	38.82	24.80	45.74	21.45
Standard Deviation	7.38	4.42	10.05	10.21	12.06	9.02	9.22	17.10	8.07
No.	94	94	94	94	94	94	94	94	94
Upper School									
Mean	25.17	14.40	39.54	33.24	41.83	42.55	30.26	57.88	28.70
Standard Deviation	10.46	7.36	16.21	9.62	11.51	10.22	11.45	18.16	9.67
No.	352	352	352	352	352	352	352	352	352
F test	2.01	2.77	2.60	1.13	1.10	1.28	1.54	1.13	1.44
t test	7.70	6.36	7.82	4.98	4.56	3.20	4.25	5.80	6.64
Signif F	*	**	**	NS	NS	NS	NS	NS	NS
Signif t	***	***	***	***	***	**	***	***	***

Significance levels $*=5\%$
$**=1\%$
$***=0.1\%$

We have then significantly greater variation of VR, NA and VN scores in the Upper School (which is not surprising in view of the entry policy of Berrymoor which discourages the very able or very weak pupils). These differences call into question the validity of the pooled variance t-tests reported in the table. Separated variance estimates of t^1 were therefore made with the following results: VR t= 9.43*** NA t=8.31*** VN t=10.14***.

The other standard deviations are not significantly different so the analyses of the differences in means by the pooled variance t-test are valid and the significance levels quoted in the table can be used with confidence.

The overall conclusion is that Berymoor pupils are significantly less able than their Upper School contemporaries on all Differential Aptitude tests. The slightly closer means on the Mechanical Reasoning test are interesting in view of the kind of courses offered at the unit.

The fact that the F ratio values are not significant for any except what might be called the 'standard academic tests' (VR, NA, VN) leads us to speculate that the counselling for Berrymoor may take too much notice of these traditional measures of aptitude or at least, of the kinds of ability for which they prognose, and too little of the specialist abilities which might be valuable to a pupil in such an establishment. Had the counsellors been looking specifically for the aptitudes which would have been valuable for the courses offered by Berrymoor,

[1] A very clear discussion of the validity of these tests is given in Parker, R. E., *Introduction Statistics for Biology* (Arnold 1975), Chapter 3. See also Chapter 8 of this report.

one would have expected the population of Berrymoor pupils to have had significantly narrower aptitude ranges on other scales as well as, if not in fact instead of, on the ones already mentioned. There is little evidence of such narrowing of the aptitude scale results.

Having seen some evidence for the fact that the counselling overall tends to relate to the 'academic aptitudes' only, we are led to ask whether the halls and grouping systems vary in the extent to which they concentrate their attentions on these measures. This is a subject to which we return in paragraph 3.5.3.

3.5.2 Numbers of Pupils choosing Berrymoor.

We look first at all of the pupils from Cohort 3 who made the choice to go to Berrymoor including those from Drayton.

Table 3.18   Numbers Choosing Berrymoor in Cohort 3.

Hall	Choosers	Non Choosers	Total
Broughton	41	77	118
Wykham	32	93	125
Stanbridge	24	96	120
Drayton	23	157	180

The effect of Drayton's quota is immediately obvious. We therefore omitted Drayton from the analysis which follows. Using the figures above we compared the numbers coming from each of the halls individually and then compared the number from the two systems (ie. Broughton plus Wykham compared with Stanbridge). Chi-squared for the individual halls was 6.73 (2 degrees of freedom, significant at 5%). The test revealed that Broughton supplied rather more pupils than would be expected in relation to the total number in that hall whereas Stanbridge supplied rather fewer. (Actual number for Broughton was 41 against an expected value of 31, whereas for Stanbridge the figures were 24 and 32 respectively.) When the systems were compared however chi-squared reached a value of only 3.64 (1 degree of freedom, not significant).

We conclude that for this year, though the halls differ, the grouping systems do not.

To add some weight to this finding, especially as we do not have the opportunity to include the second streamed community in the results, we looked at other year groups.

Table 3.19   Numbers choosing Berrymoor Cohort 2 and Cohort 4.

	Cohort/Hall	Choosers	Non-Choosers	Totals
C2	Broughton	26	99	125
	Wykham	34	100	134
	Stanbridge	29	99	128
	Chi-Squared 0.776 df=2 NS			
	Expected values for choosers: Br 29, Wy 31, St 29.			
C4	Broughton	25	91	116
	Wykham	29	135	164
	Stanbridge	24	94	118
	Chi-Squared 0.704 df=2 NS			
	Expected values for choosers : Br 23, Wy 32, St 23			

In neither case is the difference significant nor is the trend revealed by the expected values consistent (Broughton sent fewer pupils in C2, marginally more in C3 and fewer in C4 and Stanbridge sent roughly the expected numbers in C2 and C4 but fewer in C3). We can only conclude that there are year by year differences but that these can in no way be associated with grouping sytems.

3.5.3 A Comparison of the Aptitudes of the Pupils from each hall who choose Berrymoor.

In these sections, since we are comparing the quality rather than the quantity of pupils who choose Berrymoor, it seems possible to include Drayton pupils in the analysis, without undue concern for the effect of the entry policy. We have therefore done this, especially as, without the Drayton figures of the numbers for the Streamed system would have been large enough for meaningful analysis. The problem of small numbers also made it unwise to study differences within the two grouping systems.

3.5.3.1 Comparison of Aptitudes of Pupils at Berrymoor and those at Upper School/Drayton.

While Section 3.5.1 gave an overall analysis of pupils, this section attempts to compare the two grouping systems in terms of the kind of pupil who goes to Berrymoor. Section 3.5.1 showed that Berrymoor pupils seemed to be selected on the basis of overall academic ability and so it was this criterion which was used to compare the systems. Table 3.20 shows the numbers of pupils from each system who fall into the three ability ranges which are identified below, followed by the numbers, in each range, who chose Berrymoor. Chi-Squared comparisons within each range were carried out and the results are also given in this table. The three ranges were determined by reference to the pupils' percentile score on the differential aptitude test VN (Verbal+Numerical Aptitude). Since the population from which the percentiles were calculated was the whole of Cohort 3, and since this has already been shown to be a population representative of the whole ability range (see Phase One report), one can immediately interpret these ranges as dividing pupils into those who are genuinely weak academically (below 25th percentile), those who are above average (above 50th percentile) and those who are in between. As already mentioned, it is the intention of Berrymoor to provide this last group (25th to 50th percentile) with worthwhile and meaningful courses.

Table 3.20 Students who do and do not choose Berrymoor—Comparison of Aptitude Test VN between Grouping Systems.

| | | RANGES | | |
		Below 25th %tile	25th-50th %tile	Above 50th %tile
Total No	Br+Wy	45	55	111
in range	St+Dr	46	61	116
No. Choosing	Br+Wy	24	18	12
Berrymoor	St+Dr	8	16	9
Comparison : Choosers v Non-Choosers				
Chi-Squared		11.361	0.317	0.318
Signif (df)		0.1%(1)	NS(1)	NS(1)

The very high significance in the lowest aptitude range implies that a far higher proportion of the lowest ability pupils go to Berrymoor from the mixed ability system than from the streamed system. Although the difference is not significant in the highest range it is interesting to note that here again more able mixed ability pupils go to Berrymoor. One is led to the hypothesis that it may be more difficult to identify the true abilities of pupils in the mixed ability system. This is a point to which we shall return in the next section and in Chapter 6.

40

3.5.3.2 Comparison of Aptitudes of Pupils within Berrymoor.

In this section we look only at the pupils who did choose Berrymoor and seek to compare, for each aptitude test, the numbers in each of the ranges who come from the two grouping systems. This approach, which does not take full account of the actual test scores but only of the rather wide range into which a pupil's scores fall, was not seen as an ideal approach, but rather as the only one possible in the time which was available.

Table 3.21 present the raw data and the results of the statistical analysis for each Differential Aptitude Test in turn. The totals differ somewhat between one test and another because of missing data caused by answer papers which were not valid.

Table 3.21 Comparison of Aptitudes within Berrymoor.

(a) Raw Data: Numbers in each Aptitude Range for each Grouping System

Dif. Ap. Test	Below 25th %tile Br+Wy	Below 25th %tile St+Dr	25th-50th %tile Br+Wy	25th-50th %tile St+Dr	Above 50th %tile Br+Wy	Above 50th %tile St+Dr	Total Br+Wy	Total St+Dr
VN	24	8	18	16	12	9	54	33
AR	24	13	11	9	18	13	53	35
CS	22	12	11	10	21	14	54	36
MR	15	8	27	13	13	14	55	35
SR	20	13	14	12	20	9	54	34
SP	26	9	17	12	11	14	54	35
LU	21	16	21	9	12	10	54	35

(b) Analysis of data

Test	VN	AR	CS	MR	SR	SP	LU
Chi-Squared	3.69	0.62	0.82	2.76	1.33	5.68	1.68
Deg. of Freedom	2	2	2	2	2	2	2
Significance	NS	NS	NS	NS	NS	NS	NS

The overall conclusion is that the sub-groups within Berrymoor (pupils from streamed and from mixed-ability backgrounds) do not differ significantly in the way in which their numbers are divided between the three ranges on each of the aptitude tests. As the spelling result most closely approaches significance, we offer in Appendix 9, some additional figures from the Spelling analysis. It is of interest to note than in most cases (all except MR), the figures Table 3.21 show more low ability and high ability pupils from mixed ability halls choosing Berrymoor than would be expected from the total numbers in each category. This is what one would expect if it is indeed harder to accurately assess pupils in the mixed ability system.

3.5.4 Choice of Berrymoor—Conclusions.

Since the differences reported in the preceding sections are generally too small to reach statistical significance, we are led to conclude that, both in number and in quality, the pupils from the different grouping systems who choose Berrymoor are similar. Had there been significant differences we might have been able to comment on standards of counselling in the two systems, on the development of an individualistic approach to course choice, on pupils' tendency to opt away from the normal school environment or on their tendency to look towards the more adult environment of a technical college (for choice of Berrymoor could, if detailed analysis supported the idea, have been taken to indicate any of these tendencies). As it is, all that we can say with certainty is that the effects of a different grouping system in the first two years has little influence on matters such as these.

Attainment in O-Level and CSE Examinations

4.1 Introduction

Although the publication of examination results came after the official end of the research programme, we were able to put aside some time to study them and offer below the findings of this work. This is clearly an area of great importance in any comparison of grouping systems, and it is unfortunate that in this project it could not have been given the amount of attention which it deserves. Nevertheless, we have been able to compare grouping systems in relation to the results obtained by their pupils in eight 'basic' subjects, to study the results in each of four major subject areas, and to extend this second type of comparison so that we could look at high, middle and low VRQ pupils separately. We have also been able to do some work on the results of boys and girls separately.

The main findings are:

    (i)   that there were few significant differences between the VRQ and Differential Aptitude scores of pupils from the two grouping systems[1] who were entered for O-level. A similar result was found to be true for those entered for CSE.

   (ii)   that there was some evidence of better *overall* performance on the part of less able pupils from the mixed ability situation, without any lowering of the overall levels of attainment achieved by the more able.

  (iii)   that there were few significant differences between systems in the levels of attainment achieved on *individual* subjects or subject areas.

  (iv)   that the trends indicated by those results which failed to reach significant levels of difference, were usually such as to favour the mixed ability system.

   (v)   that the differences which *did* occur between systems seemed not to be restricted to any one part of the VRQ range.

  (vi)   that the boys from the two systems seemed to show larger differences in the levels of achievement reached, than did girls.

Inevitably the shortage of time has forced some omissions in the work of this chapter. We would have liked, for example, to apply covariance techniques to the results data to take account of the small differences which were apparent between the VRQ and Differential Aptitude scores of pupils from the two systems who were entered for the examinations. We feel, however, that such omissions have had only a small effect on the general findings of the chapter and it therefore contains some important results. At very least, it provides important pointers to the effects of early ability grouping on examination performance which may be of value to others who are able to follow up the effects in more detail.

---

[1] We would remind the reader that pupils from the mixed ability system remained in mixed ability teaching groups only for their first, and sometimes second, years. They were not in mixed ability groups right through to year five.

4.2 Comparisons, between Grouping Systems, of the Ability of Pupils Entered for O-level and CSE Examinations.

To ensure the correct interpretation of any differences between the results obtained by pupils from the two systems, it is important to know if the abilities of the two groups of pupils who are entered for a particular subject at a particular level, were significantly different. As a preliminary to our work on results we carried out an analysis to assess the comparability of the samples and present the findings in this section.

4.2.1 Comparability of those entering for O-level.

The abilities of the two groups, entered for O-level in a particular subject but coming from different early grouping backgrounds, were measured on VRQ and Differential Aptitude scales. There were therefore ten measurements which could be compared by means of F and t tests for each subject studied. We carried out comparisons for each of the eight 'basic' subjects referred to later in the chapter (Mathematics, English, French, Geography, History, Physics, Chemistry, Biology). There were therefore 80 F test comparisons and 80 t test comparisons involved. We found no significant differences between mean scores (as indicated by t tests), and eight significant differences between variances (as indicated by F tests). Although over the 160 tests performed, some statistical significances are not at all unexpected simply as a result of chance, there are two features which call for further comment. First, four of the significant differences of variance occurred between the two groups entered for English. On the four tests involved, (VRQ, Clerical Speed and Accuracy, Spelling, Language Usage), the differences implied that the sample of O-level English entrants from the streamed system was of wider ability than the comparable group from the mixed ability system. (The results on all tests for the O-level English groups are shown in Appendix 14.)

Secondly, the other significant differences occur, in all but one case, on VRQ tests. Often the streamed system provides a wider spread of VRQ than the mixed ability system. This is not, however, a consistent result, neither is it a trend followed in those situations in which the differences fail to reach significance. (The basic data on VRQ tests is presented in Appendix 14, Table A 14.1.)

4.2.2 Comparability of those entering for CSE.

Again the number of significant differences arising from the 160 tests was small enough to be explained simply in terms of chance. (There were two t test significances and eight F test significances.) Again there were two interesting points to consider. First, all of the 'non-VRQ' differences occurred in Physics. These may go some way towards explaining the difference in results shown in Table 4.5. We give the basic data in Appendix 14. Secondly, as at O-level, several significant differences occurred on VRQ tests. This time there was a consistent trend. Without exception the mixed ability system groups were ones with higher variance (ie. a wider range of abilities) and often lower, though not significantly lower, means.

It again appears to be more difficult to assess accurately the ability of middle VRQ pupils in the mixed ability situation. (This is a point to which we have referred in Sections 3.5.3.1, 6.2 and 6.3). Such a difficulty may well imply that a wider range of mixed ability pupils would begin a CSE course.

4.2.3 Conclusion.

With the few detailed considerations outlined above in mind, we feel that the main finding of these background ability comparisons was that there was very little difference between the groups from the two grouping systems. We can therefore look at overall differences between results gained at public examinations without the need for complicated reference back to other information. This makes the interpretation of what follows in Section 4.3 very much more straight-forward.

A similar simple approach can be applied to the differences between results in broad subject areas reported in the first part of section 4.4. When we look at *individual* subject differences we should, however, make more careful reference to the few significant differences which have been described above.

4.3 Overall Attainment.

Table 4.2 shows the number of times particular grades were achieved in the two grouping systems. The expected values, based on the same row and column totals, are also shown and comparison of the observed results with these expected values enables one to determine the way in which the grouping systems differ. It is unfortunate that the method by which these results were obtained did not make it possible to divide the top and bottom grade ranges into individual grades.

In many of the tables which follow in this chapter, chi-squared has been cal-culated to indicate the extent to which weight should be given to the differences between observed and expected results. We have, however, omitted any refer-ence to levels of significance. This is because each student has been included several times in the tables and the samples cannot therefore be thought of as entirely random.

Where the details of the analysis imply that significance levels *are* appropriate, they are quoted. Where they have not been given, the reader may find it of value to know that, for truly random samples, the minimum chi-squareds which give 5% significance are:

$$1 \text{ df} \quad \chi^2 = 3.84$$
$$2 \text{ df} \quad \chi^2 = 5.99$$
$$3 \text{ df} \quad \chi^2 = 7.81$$

Table 4.2 Overall Comparison of Examination Results

O-LEVEL Grades	1 & 2	3	4	5 & 6
Observed results				
B & W	123	109	51	96
S + D	104	110	54	127
Expected results				
B + W	111.1	107.2	51.4	109.2
S + D	115.9	111.8	53.6	113.8
Chi-Squared = 5.66 df = 3				

CSE Grades	1 & 2	3	4	5 & 6
Observed results				
B + W	117	238	223	124
S + D	223	239	254	200
Expected results				
B + W	181.6	216.6	216.6	147.1
S + D	218.4	260.4	260.4	176.9
Chi-Squared = 11.1 df = 3				

Thus the mixed ability system produces slightly fewer CSE grades 1 and 2, rather more grades 3 and 4 and many fewer bottom grades (5 and 6). By far the largest contribution to the value of chi-squared comes from this difference in the lowest grade range. We conclude that the mixed ability system produces fewer bottom grades at CSE and infer that the less able pupils do rather better if their early grouping background is a mixed ability one.

When we turn to the O-level table we see that the overall difference between the systems fails to reach such a high level. Nevertheless the trends shown by the figures are interesting. We see that the mixed ability system has fewer low grades than expected (96 compared with 109.2) and rather more top grades than expected (123 compared with 111.1). We suggest that there is no evidence here that the more able pupils do less well if they are grouped heterogeneously in their first years in the secondary school.

In Section 4.2 we showed that there were few occasions when the groups of candidates for a particular examination, who came from different grouping systems, had significantly different general abilities as measured by VRQ or Differential Aptitude Tests. We therefore feel that the overall differences in achievement which have been discussed in this section cannot be fully explained in terms of such general background-ability differences.

4.4 Achievement of all Pupils in Individual Subjects and Subject Groups

The same method as was used to assess overall performance was applied to four main subject areas. The results are shown in Tables 4.3 and 4.4, Section 4.4.1. The method was then used again on each of the eight 'basic' subjects. The results are discussed in Section 4.4.2.

4.4.1 Subject Areas
4.4.1.1 Subject Areas: Results

Table 4.3 CSE Results in Four Main Subject Areas

Subject	Observed numbers in each grade range				Expected numbers in each grade range				Chi-Squared
	1&2	3	4	5&6	1&2	3	4	5&6	
Science									
B + W	41	56	55	12	37.8	55.9	53.2	17.0	
									3.98 df = 3
S + D	28	46	42	19	31.2	46.1	43.8	14.0	
Languages									
B + W	11	14	14	7	10.8	14.0	11.4	9.8	
									2.05 df = 3
S + D	22	29	21	23	22.2	29.0	23.6	20.2	
Human Studies									
B + W	34	51	41	55	33.3	44.6	44.2	58.9	
									2.50 df = 3
S + D	43	52	61	81	43.7	58.4	57.8	77.1	
Design									
B + W	38	42	30	24	37.8	37.8	35.3	23.2	
									2.20 df = 3
S + D	53	49	55	32	53.2	53.2	49.7	32.8	

Table 4.4 O-level Results in Four Main Subject Areas

Subject	Observed numbers in each grade range				Expected numbers in each grade range				Chi-Squared
	1&2	3	4	5&6	1&2	3	4	5&6	
Languages									
B + W	11	11	12	23	8.1	10.9	11.4	26.6	
									3.01 df = 3
S + D	6	12	12	33	8.9	12.1	12.6	29.4	
Sciences									
B + W	36	38	14	24	31.7	37.3	14.8	28.1	
									2.55 df = 3
S + D	26	35	15	31	30.3	35.7	14.2	26.9	

Subject	1&2	3	4	5&6	1&2	3	4	5&6	
Human Studies									
B + W	26	13	10	18	24.4	14.5	7.7	20.4	2.22 df = 3
S + D	28	19	7	27	29.6	17.5	9.3	24.6	
Design									
B + W	19	13	4	14	18.8	14.1	5.3	11.8	2.02 df = 3
S + D	13	11	5	6	13.2	9.9	3.7	8.2	

4.4.1.2 Subject Areas: Conclusions

While none of these results show differences which produce large values of chi-squared, it is interesting to note that almost without exception there are fewer low grades at CSE in the mixed ability system than we would expect from the row and column totals in the tables used for the Chi-Squared tests. This implies that, given the number of pupils entering for, say, a Languages examination from each system and the total numbers of pupils achieving each grade, chance alone would predict more pupils from the mixed ability system in the bottom grades than actually appear there. We have already seen similar effects for overall performances in the preceding section; these results add to our understanding in that they imply that no one section of the curriculum is particularly affected by differences in the early grouping systems.

4 2 Individual Subjects

4.4.2.1 Individual Subjects and Results

Table 4.5 CSE Results for 'Basic' Subjects

Subject	Observed numbers in each grade range				Expected numbers in each grade range				Chi-Squared with valid significance
	1&2	3	4	5&6	1&2	3	4	5&6	
English									
B + W	36	47	35	6	41.8	40.8	33.5	7.8	4.29 df=3 NS
S + D	50	37	34	10	44.2	43.2	35.4	8.2	
Maths (including Arithmetic)									
B + W	17	28	48	20	20.5	25.2	41.6	25.7	5.96 df=3 NS
S + D	27	26	41	35	23.5	28.8	47.4	29.3	
Geography									
B + W	17	34	31	16	17.3	30.3	32.7	17.7	1.32 df=3 NS
S + D	20	31	39	22	19.7	34.7	37.3	20.3	
History									
B + W	17	14	8	37	15.2	13.1	10.3	37.4	1.31 df=3 NS
S + D	20	18	17	54	21.8	18.8	14.7	53.6	
Physics									
B + W	9	11	9	3	6.5	11.0	9.0	5.5	4.20 df=3 NS
S + D	4	11	9	8	6.5	11.0	9.0	5.5	
Chemistry	1&2	3	4-6		1&2	3	4-6		
B + W	7	10	21		10.4	10.4	17.2		5.16 df=2 NS
S + D	10	7	7		6.6	6.6	10.8		
Biology	1&2	3	4-6		1&2	3	4-6		
B + W	15	12	13		13.2	13.2	13.6		0.73 df=2 NS
S + D	13	16	16		14.8	14.8	15.4		
French	1-3		4-6		1-3		4-6		
B + W	8		15		13.2		9.8		6.60 df=1 NS
S + D	26		10		20.8		15.2		

The grade ranges used in Table 4.5 for Chemistry, Biology and French were adjusted so that the numbers in the expected tables were large enough for the Chi-Squared test to be valid. Similar adjustments are made in Tables 4.6—4.11.

Table 4.6 O-level Results for 'Basic' Subjects

Subject	Observed numbers in each grade range				Expected numbers in each grade range				Chi-Squared with valid significances
	1&2	3	4	5&6	1&2	3	4	5&6	
English									
B + W	12	15	8	12	13.5	15.2	6.4	11.9	1.06 df = 3 NS
S + D	20	21	7	16	18.5	20.8	8.6	16.1	
Maths									
B + W	19	19	3	5	15.2	15.7	5.6	9.6	10.24 df = 3 2.5%
S + D	11	12	8	14	14.8	15.3	5.4	9.4	
History									
B + W	14	2	7	9	11.6	4.8	5.3	10.2	5.46 df = 3 NS
S + D	10	8	4	12	12.4	5.2	5.7	10.8	
French									
B + W	8	8	6	14	5.5	6.8	5.5	18.2	4.41 df = 3 NS
S + D	4	7	6	26	6.5	8.2	6.5	21.8	
Biology									
B + W	11	12	9	6	13.5	10.7	7.4	8.4	1.79 df=3 NS
S + D	18	11	7	10	15.5	12.3	8.6	9.6	
Geography	1&2	3	4-6		1&2	3	4-6		
B + W	10	10	11		11.2	9.0	10.8		0.46 df=2 NS
S + D	15	10	13		13.8	11.0	13.2		
Chemistry									
B + W	10	17	14		7.0	19.3	14.6		3.78 df=2 NS
S + D	2	16	11		5.0	13.7	10.4		
Physics									
B + W	15	9	7		10.3	8.4	12.3		8.74 df=2 NS
S + D	6	8	18		10.7	8.6	12.7		

4.4.2.2 Individual Subjects: Conclusions

A simple conclusion which can be drawn from these individual subject results is, that though there are some exceptions, the same pattern of achievement can be detected as has been discussed before (ie. fewer bottom CSE grades from mixed ability pupils and more top O-level grades from mixed ability pupils).

In interpreting the individual subject findings more carefully however we must take account of the work of Section 4.2.

If we look first at CSE results, we should remember that mixed ability CSE candidates for all eight subjects had higher variance on VRQ tests than their streamed counterparts. This implies a wider ability range amongst the mixed ability candidates. For several subjects (Mathematics, English, Geography and Biology) mixed ability candidates also had lower mean VRQs (though the differences were not significant). In these subjects especially, the fact that mixed ability candidates achieved fewer bottom grades at CSE is of some interest. In one subject, Physics, mixed ability candidates had slightly higher mean scores on all Differential Aptitude tests and, generally, smaller variances on the tests. The slight advantage shown by mixed ability candidates in this subject is therefore, at least in part, explicable in terms of their general ability level.

At O-level the results calling for particular attention are those for Physics and Mathematics where the differences between results reached significant levels (see Table 4.6) and were in favour of the mixed ability system. This may in part be explained by the slightly higher mean and much smaller variance on VRQ tests for the mixed ability pupils who were entered for these subjects at O-level. (see Table A14.1).

Streamed pupils entering for English at O-level have slightly lower means and larger variances on VRQ and Differential Aptitude tests (see Table A14.2) so the slightly superior examination results gained by these pupils are particularly interesting.

Our interpretation of the results of Sections 4.3 and 4.4 is that differences in attainment between systems were generally small, but where they did occur, the mixed ability system benefited the less able without *any* disadvantage to the more able.

It is most important to remember than in all subjects except Mathematics and English, Banbury School pupils were taught, in years 4 and5, in groups which contained pupils from all three halls.

The mixed ability and streamed pupils were therefore prepared for their examinations by the *same* teacher. Such differences as were disclosed above cannot therefore, be attributed to differences in teacher ability. Mathematics and English groups were constructed on the basis of pupils' previous hall and the differences in these subjects could be related to teacher effectiveness.

It is not our feeling that this could be the full explanation of the differences found.

4.4.3 Other CSE subjects

Two other CSE subjects are of general interest so we show in Table 4.7 the comparisons between results from the two grouping systems for these subjects.

Table 4.7 Comparison of Results on two Additional Subjects								
Subject	Observed numbers in each grade range			Expected numbers in each grade range				Chi-Squared
Arithmetic **CSE**	1-3	4	5&6	1-3	4	5&6		
B + W	20	30	14	18.4	28.2	17.4		
S + D	14	22	18	15.6	23.8	14.6		1.96 df=2 NS
Sciences for the less able (Rural Studies, Health Science, Secondary Science)								
CSE	1&2	3	4	5&6	1&2	3	4	5&6
B + W	10	23	18	3	6.7	21.5	20.2	5.5
S + D	1	12	15	6	4.3	13.5	12.8	3.5

7.96 df=3 5%

In both of these subjects the mixed ability system produces more top and fewer bottom grades.

4.4.4 Conclusions

We have shown that some of the individual subject differences can be understood, and perhaps in part, explained, by differences in the general ability of the pupils from the two systems who enter for those subjects. Nevertheless, there were some subject differences, albeit ones which failed to reach statistical significance, which could not be explained in this way. These, together with the general trends which were common to most subjects and to all subject areas, lead us to suppose that there were some small differences between the levels of achievement reached from the two grouping systems, which were not simply the result of differences betwen the background abilities of the pupils involved, or of differences in the teaching which they received.

The trends which therefore remain unexplained, and which we suggest may be related to early grouping differences, are:

    i)   that fewer bottom CSE grades were achieved by mixed ability pupils (which implies perhaps that less able pupils do rather better if they come from a mixed ability system).

    ii)   that more top O-level grades are achieved by mixed ability pupils (which implies perhaps that more able pupils are not handicapped by coming from a mixed ability system).

4.4.5 "Within-System" Differences

Before looking more closely at differences between grouping systems by comparing the performance of smaller sub-groups of pupils, we turn our attention to comparisons made between the performance of pupils from the two halls which make up each grouping system. If large differences had been detected on these comparisons it would have been hard to interpret the results so far discussed, in terms of the effect of the grouping system from which the pupils came. As it is, Table 4.8, which for brevity shows only the values of Chi-Squared obtained in the 'within-system' comparisons, provides evidence for the fact that most differences between halls within a system are small.

What is more, unlike the comparisons between systems, the data from which the Chi-Squared values were calculated shows no general trends. This similarity between the halls within each grouping system adds some weight to the idea that differences between the pair of halls which make up each system are related to those systems, and are not merely the result of idiosyncratic differences which might be expected between any communities.

Table 4.8   Within System Comparisons of Exam Results Obtained by Pupils

Subject Group	Chi-Squared within Streamed System St v Dr	Chi-Squared within Mixed Ability System Br v Wy
O LEVEL RESULTS		
Languages	0.002 df = 1	0.84 df = 3
Design	5.03 df = 1	1.22 df = 2
Human Studies	2.90 df = 2	3.08 df = 3
Sciences	4.10 df = 3	14.10 df = 3
CSE RESULTS		
Languages	2.08 df = 3	0.05 df = 1
Design	0.86 df = 3	5.20 df = 3
Science	2.30 df = 3	3.77 df = 3
Human Studies	2.60 df = 3	1.85 df = 3

In studying the results in this table it should be remembered that, over sixteen tests one five per cent significance may well arise purely as a result of chance. It is perhaps interesting to note that the difference which gives rise to the largest chi[2] (on science results at O-level) comes about because Wykham Hall, the most committed to mixed ability organisation in years 1 and 2, has similar numbers of grades 1 and 2, more grade 3 and fewer grades 4 to 6 than Broughton.

4.5 Comparison of Examination Results in relation to VRQ Ranges

The levels of attainment reached by the most able and least able is a matter of great concern in the debate on mixed ability teaching. It deserves more attention than we were able to give it in the necessarily sketchy survey which we were able to do of examination results. Nevertheless, we were able to analyse performance of three VRQ ranges of pupils separately and present the findings in this section.

4.5.1 High VRQ Pupils

Pupils whose VRQ scores were above 110 were studied and differences in examination grades were subjected to Chi-Squared tests in the way described in Section 4.4. Table 4.9 shows the results of these tests.

Table 4.9 Chi-Squared Comparisons of Results Achieved by High VRQ Pupils in the two Grouping Systems

Subject	Observed Numbers in each grade Range				Chi-Squared
	1&2	3	4	5&6	
O LEVEL					
Languages					
B + W	8	6	4	13	
					2.93 df = 3
S + D	4	11	9	13	
Science					
B + W	25	14	10	14	
					3.82 df = 3
S + D	18	20	6	8	
Design	1-3	4-6			
B + W	13	5			
					0.16 df = 1
S + D	8	3			
Human St.	1&2	3	4-6		
B + W	17	5	13		
					2.03 df = 2
S + D	21	13	14		
CSE	1&2	3	4-6		
Languages					
B + W	4	9	8		
					3.27 df = 2
S + D	9	11	4		
Design					
B + W	11	6	5		
					2.07 df = 2
S + D	10	5	11		
Science					
B + W	18	12	4		
					0.56 df = 2
S + D	10	7	4		
Human St.					
B + W	11	8	7		
					0.63 df = 2
S + D	14	6	7		

There are, therefore, no large differences between the levels of attainment reached by the high VRQ pupils. In all subject areas at O-level the numbers of students with grades 1 or 2 (Actual grades A or B) was higher than the expected number in the case of the mixed ability system.

4.5.2 Mid VRQ Pupils

The results of an identical analysis for pupils of VRQ 86-109 are shown in Table 4.10.

Table 4.10 Chi-Squared Comparisons of Results Achieved by Mid VRQ Pupils in the two Grouping Systems

Subject	Observed numbers in each Grade Range				Chi-Squared
	1&2	3	4-6		
O LEVEL					
Design					
B + W	10	7	12		
					0.38 df = 2
S + D	7	7	8		
Human St.					
B + W	9	7	14		
					1.25 df = 2
S + D	7	6	20		
Languages	1-3	4-6			
B + W	8	13			
					2.96 df = 1
S + D	3	22			
Sciences	1&2	3	4	5&6	
B + W	11	23	3	9	
					9.51 df = 3
S + D	8	15	9	21	
CSE					
Languages					
B + W	7	5	5	6	
					1.91 df = 3
S + D	11	17	17	20	
Design					
B + W	21	31	21	10	
					2.34 df = 3
S + D	40	35	31	18	
Science					
B + W	21	37	40	6	
					4.80 df = 3
S + D	17	34	27	13	
Human St.					
B + W	20	35	31	35	
					0.73 df = 3
S + D	28	40	40	52	

The only large difference is for mid-VRQ pupils on O-level science. The fact that the trends fit the now familiar pattern of more top grades from the mixed ability system is of particular importance in view of the earlier finding (Section 3.3.3) that more middle ability pupils chose science in this system. There is no evidence here which would suggest that this additional choice was ill advised (ie. that the additional pupils choosing were unsuitable for the courses). This is especially so as the CSE figures for mid-VRQ results in science also fit the pattern.

4.5.3 Low VRQ Pupils

The last group is of those pupils whose VRQs were below 85. Since very few were entered for O-level no results can be given. Again very small numbers (2 in Broughton and Wykham, 6 in Stanbridge and Drayton) were entered for CSE languages and so this subject group has also been omitted from the table which follows.

Table 4.11 Chi-Squared Comparisons of Results Achieved by low VRQ Pupils from the two Grouping Systems

Subject	Observed numbers in each Grade Range				Chi-Squared
Design	1&2	3	4	5&6	
B + W	6	5	7	11	
					4.50 df = 3
S + D	3	9	17	10	
Sciences	1&2	3	4-6		
B + W	18	12	4		
					0.56 df = 2
S + D	10	7	4		
Human St.	1-3	4	5&6		
B + W	11	8	15		
					4.08 df = 2
S + D	7	16	27		

Again no large differences are to be found. In view of the discussion of science results above, it is interesting to note that again the figures for low VRQ pupils fit the pattern which we have set out before.

4.5.4 Summary

The general conclusion which can be drawn from these results is that there is no single section of the ability range for which early grouping systems have a statistically significant effect on examination results. The trends mentioned in Section 4.4 seem to be in evidence in all three sections which were studied. We feel that it would be most useful if a study of the very able and the very weak were to be undertaken. Certainly the results which we have presented cannot be said to prove that pupils of exceptional ability or of very low ability are unaffected by grouping systems, for the VRQ ranges which we used were too wide to isolate such students.

We did compare the results of the top 5% of the Banbury and Drayton School populations (VRQs above 120) and found no significant differences between grouping systems. We would point out that the sample consists of few individuals and so we hesitate to place any importance on the finding. Any additional work on this problem would have to involve many schools so that the numbers involved were sufficiently large.

4.5.6 Correlation of Examination Results with General Scholastic Ability

The Differential Aptitude Test sub-scale VN provided us with an up-to-date measure of the general scholastic ability of the pupils. We show below the results of calculations to find the correlation between this measure and the examination results achieved. The correlations were found for the eight 'basic' subjects. O-level and CSE results were treated separately.

So that the correlation coefficients which were calculated could be more easily interpreted, we scored examination results so that a high score corresponded to a high level of achievement. This method of scoring is the reverse of that used elsewhere in this chapter.

Table 4.12 Correlations Between Examination Results and Differential Aptitude Scale VN

Subject	Broughton + Wykham	Stanbridge + Drayton	Broughton + Wykham	Stanbridge + Drayton
	O LEVEL		CSE	
English	0.465(47)*	0.460(64)*	0.240(124)*	0.518(131)*
Maths	0.224(46)	0.435(45)*	0.497(49)*	0.578(76)*
Geography	0.025(31)	0.419(38)*	0.495(101)*	0.535(114)*
History	0.111(32)	0.381(35)*	0.439(77)*	0.389(110)*
French	0.354(36)*	0.440(43)*	0.236(23)	0.496(37)*
Physics	0.415(31)*	0.660(33)*	0.654(32)*	0.289(33)
Chemistry	0.442(41)*	0.507(29)*	0.653(38)*	0.213(24)
Biology	0.423(40)*	0.322(46)*	0.436(40)*	0.456(45)*

*significant at 5% or higher levels
figure in parentheses = number of pupils involved

It is interesting to note that in 11 of the 16 cases, there is a higher level of correlation between general scholastic ability and examination results for the pupils from the streamed system. In Table 2.7 of the report on the first phase of the project, Dr. Newbold has established that there were very high correlations (all above 0.6) between primary school estimates and VRQ. Since primary school estimates are used to place pupils in their streamed groups, we can infer that streaming attaches labels to pupils, and these labels are related to their VRQ. The Differential Aptitude scale VN is highly correlated with other tests of general scholastic ability such as VRQ[1]: so that our findings suggest that the pupils who do well in the streamed system are those who were labelled as able pupils from the first year. The particularly interesting feature is that we have already shown that mixed ability pupils achieve rather more top O-level grades than streamed pupils. So we can suggest that when they are freed from the effects of early labels by a mixed ability system of organisation, the pupils who succeed in public examinations are greater in number and have a wider range of VRQs scores.

It is tempting in view of this evidence to suggest that the mixed ability system allows for greater exploitation of all kinds of academic potential, whereas the streamed system does more to confine success to those sorts of pupil who score well on VRQ-type tests.

4.6 Achievement of Boys and Girls in the two Grouping Systems

We were able to show in Section 3.3.4 that the differences between the patterns of subject choice in the two systems were greater for girls than for boys. The systems therefore, in this respect, affected boys and girls to differing extents. This prompted us to investigate whether or not the same sort of differential effect on the sexes was apparent in the examination results obtained. Table 4.13 shows the results of comparisons, between systems, of examination results for boys alone and for girls alone.

Table 4.13 Examinations Results Comparisons, Boys and Girls Separately

Subject	Chi-Squared between Grouping Systems	
	Boys only	Girls only
O LEVEL		
Human St.	5.58 df = 3	0.74 df = 2
Design	2.04 df = 2	0.24 df = 1
Languages	8.42 df = 1	0.16 df = 3
Science	6.28 df = 3	1.61 df = 3
CSE		
Human St.	3.39 df = 3	0.19 df = 3
Design	1.23 df = 3	0.65 df = 3
Languages	6.00 df = 2	6.59 df = 2
Science	6.33 df = 3	3.37 df = 3

[1] Table 44 of the Differential Aptitude Test Manual (op cit) shows these correlations and indicates that 39 of the 46 correlations measured were above 0.70.

53

It is interesting to note that the values of Chi-Squared, and therefore the extent of the differences between observed and expected results, are almost always larger for the boys. For O-level languages, the tables from which these figures were derived show more mixed ability boys in the upper grades than streamed boys. The CSE languages result is of considerable interest as the tables show more mixed ability boys in the upper grades than streamed boys but more streamed girls in these upper grades than mixed ability girls. There is a distinct indication here, that needs to be followed up by other work, that the two grouping systems affect the achievement of boys and girls in different ways.

In interpreting these findings it is interesting to call to mind the differences which we revealed between the Differential Aptitude scores of boys and girls on the Language Usage sub-test. (These differences were reported in Tables 3.7 and 3.8). We were able to show that girls have higher Language Usage scores than boys. Boys were shown above to do better on languages at O and CSE level if they were, in their first years, in streamed halls. It seems in this case that the inherently less able boys are better able to develop their abilities in a mixed ability system (where perhaps they are not always outclassed by the majority of the girls in their teaching groups). The more able girls, however, benefit from the streamed system (perhaps as a result of increased competition?). Since Differential Aptitude differences were also discovered in those aptitudes which might be thought to be related to scientific ability, it is interesting now to turn to the differences in performance of boys and girls in the sciences. Again at CSE one could follow through the same kind of argument as that put forward for languages, for the girls, this time the inherently less able group, seem to do rather better from the mixed ability system. (They score more grades 1-3 and fewer grades 4-6 than expected). The picture is rather less clear this time, however, as the boys also appear to perform better in the sciences (at both O-level and CSE) if they come from the mixed ability system. Clearly more work is needed to turn these interesting conjectures into anything more substantial.

4.7 General Comments

In concluding this chapter, we feel that it is important to draw attention to the fact that public examinations, while providing an assessment of pupils which is of the utmost importance, fail to provide a full assessment of the whole spectrum of abilities which a school might aim to develop in its pupils. They can provide only partial and indirect evidence on, for example, pupils' creativity, powers of logical thought, aptitude for divergent thinking, and level of moral and social understanding. While this does nothing to reduce the importance of the work reported here, it does emphasise that much remains to be done if a full understanding of the effects of mixed ability and streamed groupings on *all* aspects of achievement is to be obtained.

The years beyond 16

5. Introduction

It was seen as important to the completeness of the project that some comment be made on the decisions made by pupils at the end of the compulsory period of their education. With this in mind, the project has made a study of the broad areas of choice involved (eg. by comparing the pupils who opt for continued education at school, continued education at a technical college or employment) and, where possible, a more detailed study within those areas. We have therefore studied sixth form subject choice. We made an attempt to study the nature of choices within employment, but the data consisted of very small numbers and was anyway rather unreliable, for it is difficult to say what kind of job a pupil has if his record merely shows that he has joined an engineering company. He may be a clerical officer, an apprentice engineer, a cleaner or a maintenance man. Enquiries could of course be made to deepen our knowledge but, as the work necessarily fell outside the year allotted for the research, time was very short indeed, and such enquiries would have been totally unrealistic.

In this section the project has relied to a considerable extent on the data provided by the careers staff within the school to whom we are most grateful for the cooperation which we have received.

Data for Drayton was only available for the pupils who transferred to the Upper School.

The main findings are as follows:

i) the systems showed few differences in connection with the numbers or quality of pupils who opted for each of the three broad alternatives of Upper School, Technical College or Job, and no conclusive trends.

ii) tests of career aspiration failed to show any difference between systems with regard to the areas of career interest for which the pupils showed preference.

iii) for pupils choosing a sixth form career in the Upper School, vestiges of the subject choice differences shown in chapter 3 of this report, did continue to make themselves apparent.

5.2 An overall study

The first stage was to count the numbers of pupils from each system who opted for each of the three broad categories, "Job, Technical College or Upper School." The results of this count are given in Table 5.1. To the data presented there, we can add the fact that 17 Drayton pupils were known to have joined the Upper School at the time when the data was collected (14th May 1977).

Table 5.1 General Areas of 16+ Choice			
	Upper School	Technical College	Employment
Broughton Hall	25	14	28
Wykham Hall	28	24	29
Stanbridge Hall	28	29	23
Chi-Squared = 4.801 Degrees of freedom = 4 Not Significant			

Thus in general terms there can be seen to be no overall bias in the way in which pupils from the systems choose to spend their first years after compulsory education.

Analysis of the systems (Br+Wy against St) and of the two halls in the mixed ability system was also carried out, though on the basis of slightly less complete data. This analysis also showed no significant differences (Between systems $\chi^2 = 2.324$ df = 2 NS; Between halls in the mixed ability system $\chi^2 = 0.214$ df = 2 NS).

The next stage in this introductory study was to compare the abilities of those from each system who had chosen each of the three options. This was done by calculating the mean VRQ of each group of pupils. The results are presented in table 5.2. The numbers shown in the columns on the right are slightly smaller than those in Table 5.1 because pupils whose VRQ was not known or omitted from Table 5.2.

Table 5.2 Mean VRQs of Pupils opting for Upper School, Technical College or Employment

	Mean Upper Sch.	Tech	Job	Standard Deviation Upper Sch.	Tech	Job	Number Upper Sch.	Tech	Job
Broughton	111.54	96.36	98.88	11.10	11.61	10.78	24	14	26
Wykham	109.48	98.62	97.64	12.44	14.05	13.06	27	24	28
Stanbridge	108.64	93.10	91.00	9.70	13.92	16.15	28	29	23
Drayton	112.18	—	—	9.01	—	—	17	—	—
Br. & Wy.	110.45	97.79	98.24	11.76	13.09	11.92	51	38	54
St. & Dr.	109.98	—	—	9.50	—	—	45	—	—

Table 5.3 shows the F and t-test results which were obtained by comparing halls within each category of choice.

Table 5.3 Statistical Analysis of each Category of Choice

(i) UPPER SCHOOL

	F ratio	df 1	df 2	Significance	t-test	df	Significance
Br/Wy	1.256	26	23	NS	0.621	49	NS
St/Dr	1.159	27	16	NS	1.218	43	NS
B+W/S+D	1.532	50	44	NS	0.214	94	NS

(ii) TECHNICAL COLLEGE

	F ratio	df 1	df 2	Significance	t-test	df	Significance
Br/Wy	1.464	23	13	NS	0.508	36	NS
B+W/S	1.313	28	37	NS	1.414	65	NS

(iii) EMPLOYMENT

	F ratio	df 1	df 2	Significance	t-test	df	Significance
Br/Wy	1.468	27	25	NS	0.379	52	NS
B+W/S	1.836	22	53	5%	2.186	75	5%

The only significant differences to arise appear in the 'employment' section of the table where mixed ability pupils entering employment are found to have a higher mean (Br+Wy 98.24, St 91.0) but a smaller standard deviation (Br+Wy 11.92, St 16.15). It could be supposed, in an attempt to explain the smaller mean in the streamed system, that low ability pupils from this system carried with them a poor image of themselves from their early form groupings, would tend to avoid a college course (on the basis that they felt themselves to be unfit for any kind of further education) and opted for employment. If it were assumed that there was a 'basic group' of moderate ability pupils in each system who would anyway opt for employment, the addition of a larger number of lower ability pupils to the 'employment group' in the streamed system, which would be brought about by a process such as that described, could, at the same time, lower the mean and increase the range (and therefore the standard deviation). However, such an explanation is called into question by the similarity of the samples who *do* opt for the technical college from the two systems. Further work, on a larger sample would be needed to unearth any genuine causes of effects of this kind.

5.3 A detailed study of the employment option

This fell into two sections. First we assessed the career aspiration of the whole Upper School population irrespective of whether or not they intended to seek employment at the end of their fifth year. Data for this assessment was provided by the careers department and was derived from tests which they use, as part of their normal programme of careers education. Unfortunately data for Berrymoor pupils was lost during a move from one careers office to another. Secondly, we attempted to follow pupils through to their actual career choices. It was this attempt which fell foul of the difficulties already described in the introduction to this chapter. The results which were obtained are presented in Appendix 10.

5.31 Career Aspiration

5.3.1.1 Introduction

The test used by the careers department to assess pupils career preference was the Applied Psychology Unit (APU) Occupational Interests Guide. This divides careers into eight categories. Each category is described, not in general 'careers brochure' terms, but rather in terms of short descriptions of activities which would actually go on in jobs within the category. Using these descriptions, one category is juxtaposed with another and the pupil is asked to say in which kind of activity he would prefer to take part.

Each category is juxtaposed with every other (28 pairings) and each pairing is repeated four times in the test which therefore has 112 items. These are grouped into two sections of 56 items each and scores on these two equivalent sections can be used to assess the consistency of a pupil's answers. In the work which follows, only results which meet the APU criteria for adequate consistency are used.

It is important to realise that at no time in the test is the pupil asked to assess whether or not he is actually able to do a particular type of job but simply whether he prefers it to another. A consequence of this is that his preference may be completely unrealistic. A second and equally important consideration is that while he may prefer one category to another he may actually like neither of them. The style of the test implies that pupils will take no account of such things as pay, hours or job conditions when they do the questions. These comments make it impossible to use the test results as a predictor of which career a pupil will ultimately choose, though they do give a counsellor an idea of the areas towards which he might be guided and and away from which he should be drawn. They also give us some insight into the career interests which might be fostered by a particular grouping system.

The eight categories to which the test refers, together with brief descriptions of each are given below.

Scientific	(SCI)	—interest in knowing the how and why of things particularly in the realm of natural sciences.
Social Services	(SOC)	—helping people for their own sake, those activities in which the person is the end and not the means.
Clerical/Sales	(C/S)	—doing clerical/secretarial work and also meeting and dealing with people in shops and offices.
Literary	(LIT)	—the use of words and manipulation of verbal concepts
Artistic	(ART)	—painting, sculpture and *visual* art in all forms.
Computations	(COMP)	—systematic recording and classifying of information and performing mathematical operations on data.

| | Practical | (PRAC) | —constructive activities which involve working with machines or making things with the hands. |
| | Outdoor | (OUT) | —working in the open air, mainly with plants and animals. |

5.3.1.2 Analysis of test results

Table 5.4 Numbers by Hall in each APU Category

HALL	CATEGORY	SCI	SOC	C/S	LIT	ART	COMP	PRAC	OUT
Broughton		29	26	21	5	20	23	22	29
Wykham		20	26	28	9	37	14	33	34
Stanbridge		26	24	20	9	17	12	20	21
TOTAL		75	76	69	23	74	49	75	84

The general spread of aspiration is of interest (particularly the very low-choice of literary and computational careers) but what is of real concern from the point of view of the project is the existence of differences (if any) between the grouping systems. In order that we might investigate such differences we compared numbers choosing particular categories in each grouping system

The results together with the results of chi-squared tests done on them, are given in Table 5.5 below.

Table 5.2 Comparison of Grouping Systems in relation to the popularity of APU categories

Category	Hall	Number Choosing	Number not choosing	Chi-Squared	Significance
SCIENCE					
	B+W	49	126		
	S	26	42	1.948 df=1	NS
SOCIAL					
	B+W	52	123		
	S	24	44	0.473 df=1	NS
CLERICAL/SALES					
	B+W	49	126		
	S	20	48	0.004 df=1	NS
LITERARY					
	B+W	14	161		
	S	9	59	1.015 df=1	NS
ARTISTIC					
	B+W	57	118		
	S	17	51	0.992 df=1	NS
COMPUTATIONAL					
	B+W	37	138		
	S	12	56	0.186 df=1	NS
PRACTICAL					
	B+W	55	120		
	S	20	48	0.023 df=1	NS
OUTDOOR					
	B+W	63	112		
	S	21	47	0.363 df=1	NS

Differences between Broughton and Wykham Halls were checked in a similar fashion and again, no significant differences were found.

The entire sample of APU tests was then divided according to VRQ and similar checks done on low, middle and high VRQ ranges separately. Again no significant differences were found between systems. The results of this work are appended. (Appendix 8).

Finally, in an attempt to differentiate between the APU results of pupils of differing VRQ, we measure the mean VRQ of the pupils in each APU category. A student was counted as being 'in an APU category' if that category was his first or second most popular area of career interest.

Table 5.6 Mean VRQ of pupils in each APU CATEGORY

CATEGORY	HALL	MEAN	ST. DEV.	NO
SCI	B+W	103.2	14.0	46
	S	99.0	14.2	26
SOC	B+W	98.0	13.4	48
	S	96.8	13.7	23
C/S	B+W	94.5	11.2	49
	S	97.1	14.9	19
LIT	B+W	104.0	12.6	14
	S	100.7	14.5	9
ART	B+W	99.8	12.8	56
	S	96.5	15.0	17
COMP	B+W	110.4	15.8	37
	S	106.0	14.5	12
PRAC	B+W	96.9	14.7	51
	S	95.9	13.6	19
OUTDOOR	B+W	98.1	13.6	59
	S	95.3	11.1	20

Again these results are of some intrinsic interest but to compare systems it was necessary to compare these means to see if the differences between them were significant. This was done by means of F and t tests. These tests failed to uncover any significant differences.

The results are quoted below:

Table 5.7 Statistical comparison of grouping systems using mean VRQ in each APU category

Category	F Value	Degrees of freedom		t value	Degrees of freedom
Scientific	1.020	25	45	1.233	70
Social	1.050	22	47	0.362	69
Clerical Sales	1.766	18	48	0.782	66
Literary	1.320	8	13	0.585	21
Artistic	1.381	16	55	0.898	71
Computional	1.195	36	11	0.853	47
Practical	1.162	50	18	0.260	68
Outdoor	1.513	58	19	0.821	77

All results fail to reach significant levels

The overwhelming conclusion is that early grouping systems affect neither the number nor the overall ability of the pupils opting for particular categories. It would be an interesting extension of the work to see if Differential Aptitude test results could be used to predict either career area preference or indeed, final career choice. Since this did not fit easily with the main aim of grouping system comparisons, it was an avenue which we felt unable to explore in this study.

5.4 Sixth Form Subject Choice

The process by which pupils moving from year five to year six go about the task of selecting the courses which they will follow, is very similar to that described before in connection with fourth year subject choice. Clearly the subjects on offer, the formal constraints on choice and the guidance available from staff will vary, but the only difference in the process, which is relevant to our present interests, is that Drayton can this time be included in the analysis as if it were still just another hall of Banbury School. This is so because Drayton has no separate sixth form and pupils wishing to follow A level courses must transfer to Banbury, and therefore make use of exactly the same course offers as pupils who have spent their five years in Banbury School. In Table 5.8 we present the numbers of pupils from each system choosing particular course at A-level, together with comparisons of the two grouping systems. Since the numbers involved are often small, the Fisher Exact Probability has been used in most cases instead of the chi-squared test.

Table 5.8 Numbers Choosing A-Level Courses

Course	Choosers Broughton + Wykham	Stanbridge + Drayton	Significance of difference between systems	Fisher Test Result
Total Nos	41	39		
One Sci	7	7	NS	.6544
Two Sci	13	9	NS	.2702
Three Sci	4	1	NS	.1955
Biology	14	9	NS	.1989
Chemistry	19	10	5% (B+W more choice)	.0488
Physics	11	19	NS	.4492
No Science	17	22	NS ($\chi^2=1.771$ df$=1$)	
Maths	19	7	1% (B+W more choice)	.0063
English	12	18	NS (S+D more choice)	.0919
French	5	5	NS	.6634
One Human St.	15	13	NS	.4722
Two Human St.	2	7	NS (B+D more choice)	.0662
Geog	7	13	NS (S+D more choice)	.0774
History	8	8	NS	.6522

There are clear vestiges here of the trends reported at fourth year level. Fewer streamed pupils choose two or three sciences, more choose no science. More streamed pupils choose Human Studies (especially Geography). The results on Maths (more from the mixed ability system) and English (more from the streamed system) are new as the style of constraint imposed on choice at fourth year level made it impossible for us to study Maths and English choice at this stage.

It is perhaps difficult to believe that differences as marked as those reported above, can be the result of differences in grouping system years earlier in a pupil's school career. However since all of the trends (even the insignificant ones) are in the same direction as those discovered in year four subject choice and since, by detailed study (including the work on the then separate Drayton situation) these were linked to grouping system, it seems even harder to believe that these differences in sixth form choice are *not* the result of these early systems of grouping.

Since there is no evidence that mixed ability pupils perform less well, (see Chapter 4), these results could have deep implications in terms of the balance of the academic disciplines studied at A-level and perhaps therefore even of differences beyond that! This work was completed by a study of the kinds of pupils who choose subjects from the two grouping systems. To do this we divided those who chose each subject into VRQ ranges (Above 116 and Others). We counted the number in each range for each system and repeated this for each subject separately. On comparing the systems no results which even approached significance were found. (See Appendix 11). There is therefore no evidence that the extra pupils choosing subjects from one system or the other are in any way less suitable for A-level study.

60

Prognosis

6.1 Introduction.

In describing the system of subject choice in Chapter Three, we mentioned that members of staff who teach in the third year, each make an assessment of the potential shown by every pupil. This assessment is intended to be an aid to the third year form teacher who guides the pupil through the complexities of the choice process. It could be supposed that, in the streamed system, it is easy for the staff to accept the label attached to each child by the form group in which he is placed and that, as a result, individual strengths and weaknesses might not be detected. In the mixed ability system however, there are no such convenient form labels and each pupil has to be considered as an individual. There is, then, the interesting possibility that the nature of the grouping system may directly affect the way in which prognosis decisions are made by the staff and that there may, therefore, be a difference in the accuracy of the prognosis which are produced.

We checked on the accuracy of prognosis in the two systems of grouping by comparing the prognosis with the examination results in the corresponding subjects. In this study we looked at CSE and O-level separately.

The same kind of argument as that set out above could also be applied to the form teachers as they try to help pupils to make their subject choice decisions. It might be supposed that, in the streamed system, with the convenient form label as a guide, form teachers would pay less attention to the prognosis slips on each child and offer advice instead on the grounds that such a subject is or is not suitable for a pupil in, for example, 'the top stream'.

We have therefore compared the use of prognosis in the guidance of subject choice and present that analysis in the later part of the chapter.

The main findings of this chapter are:

- (i) that in both grouping systems prognosis was slightly more accurate for those students who take CSE examinations than they are for those who take O-levels.
- (ii) that there was no *significant* difference between the level of accuracy achieved in the two grouping systems.
- (iii) trends indicate that prognosis was slightly less acurate in the mixed ability system, especially at CSE level.
- (iv) there appears to be no significant difference in the extend to which prognosis was used in counselling in both systems.

It should be noted that prognosis data was not available for Drayton School students.

6.2 Accuracy of Prognosis.

The prognosis scale used during the pupils' third year was a six point scale. The categories to which staff are asked to assign each of the pupils whom they teach were as follows:

- (i) Capable of study beyond O-level
- (ii) Definitely capable of O-level, though not perhaps of study beyond this
- (iii) Borderline O-level, definite CSE candidate

(iv)   Definite CSE candidate, though not capable of O-level

(v)   Probable non-exam candidate, though possibly suitable for CSE

(vi)   Definite non-exam student.

The first step in analysing the data was to draw up tables, which could be subjected to Gamma (γ) tests, in order that the degree of association betwen prognosis and examination result could be determined. These tables, produced for O-level and CSE results separately, are given in Appendix 13. The results of the Gamma tests are shown in Table 6.1.

As in Chapter Four, students' data may appear several times in some of the following tables. Thus the samples under study may be such that they cannot be treated as random. [One could, perhaps, argue that the data offered in these tables is based not on a sample of pupils, (in which case pupils' data appears several times—once for each subject) but on a sample of teacher/pupil combinations (in which case each combination provides only one piece of data for the table)].

To avoid what might be considered a spurious reference to levels of significance we have omitted them from the appropriate tables.

Table 6.1 Degree of Association between Prognosis Data and Examination Results.

Hall	Gamma		Hall	Gamma
O-LEVEL			CSE	
Br	0.46		Br	0.35
Wy	0.24		Wy	0.38
St	0.33		St	0.48
Br+Wy	0.34		Br+Wy	0.35

If the samples used in the above table were truly random all of the Gamma values quoted would reach a 1% level of significance.

It is encouraging that large levels of association are reached in all cases. Indeed it would be disturbing if this were not the case for the implication would be that teachers' assessments of pupils are little better than those which could be generated by random allocation of prognosis grades. Nevertheless, it is interesting to note that at O-level, Wykham Hall, the most committed to mixed ability teaching, produces less accurate prognoses (as shown by the smaller value of Gamma), and that at CSE, the mixed ability system overall produces less accurate prognosis (Br+Wy, $\gamma=0.35$; St, $\gamma=0.48$).

In an attempt to investigate this further we counted up the number of 'correct' prognoses in each system, and used chi-squared tests to reveal significant differences between them. The criteria used to determine whether or not a prognosis was 'correct' are set out below.

Table 6.2 Definition of Correct Prognoses.

O-LEVEL			CSE	
Prognosis	Exam. Grade		Prognosis	Exam. Grade
1	A		1	1
2	A or B		2	1
3	A or B or C		3	1
4	D		4	2 or 3
5	E		5	4 or 5
6	U		6	U

This definition of what was to be taken as a 'correct' prognosis was necessarily rather arbitrary. Nevertheless, as it was to be used as the basis of a comparison between two systems rather than as a measure of the precision of the prognosis system overall, this arbitrary nature did not prove to be too much of a handicap.

Table 6.3 Comparison of the Accuracy of Prognosis between Halls and Grouping Systems.

Hall	No of 'correct' Prognoses	No of 'incorrect' Prognoses	% correct	Chi-Squared Tests
O-LEVEL				
Br	41	136	23	Within mixed ability (Br v Wy)
Wy	57	139	29	$\chi^2=1.39$ df$=1$
St	49	105	32	Between system (Br+Wy v St)
				$\chi^2=1.40$ df$=1$
CSE				
Br	122	169	42	Within mixed ability (Br v Wy)
Wy	90	223	29	$\chi^2=10.91$ df$=1$
St	123	216	36	Between systems (Br+Wy v St)
				$\chi^2=0.09$ df$=1$

Minimum χ^2 for 5% significance$=3.84$ (df$=1$) for random samples.

From the values in the '% correct' column, supported by the chi-squared figures, we can see that at O-level and CSE there is little difference between grouping systems in the number of correct prognoses that they produce. At CSE however there is a very large difference between Broughton and Wykham Halls, with Wykham, the most committed to mixed ability, producing far fewer accurate prognoses. There appears to be some indication therefore that in the mixed ability system it is rather harder to assess the abilities of pupils, particularly those of middle ability (ie. those taking CSE examinations).

In relating the results of Table 6.3 to those of Table 6.1 one should remember that Table 6.3 takes no account of how much the incorrect prognoses differ from the values which would be expected if the prognosis were correct. There is, therefore, no contradiction in the fact that Wykham produces a slightly higher proportion of correct prognoses (57/196 for Wykham compared with 41/177 for Broughton at O-level) and yet has a lower level of association between prognosis and result (Wy $\gamma=0.24$; Br $\gamma=0.46$).

It is of general interest to note that the overall proportion of correct prognoses in both systems is rather low (of the order of 30%). This is perhaps lower than most teachers would expect and certainly lower than all would hope. There is perhaps an indication that more work should be done to enable an improvement in this aspect of student assessment to be made. We return to this point in Appendix 5 and Chapter 9.

6.3 The Relationship of Prognosis to VRQ.

There were some indications in the work described above, that prognosis might be less easy to do accurately in a mixed ability situation. In order that we might further investigate this idea we decided to study the kinds of prognosis made in each hall for pupils in specific VRQ ranges. In this way we hope to reveal whether there was a particular kind of pupil for whom prognosis was especially difficult in the mixed ability situation.

So that it might be easier to relate prognosis scores and VRQ ranges we decided, in this section only, to score the prognosis forms so that a good prognosis had a score of 6 and a poor prognosis a score of 1. This had the effect of ensuring that a high VRQ score should be related to a high prognosis score and therefore made the study of the numbers in Table 6.4 more straightforward. It should

63

however be remembered that this system of scoring is the reverse of that used in the rest of this chapter.

Table 6.4 shows the results of the analysis. The mean prognosis scores for each VRQ range were found for each of the grouping systems. These mean scores were then compared by F and t tests. The results of these tests were shown in the lower part of the table.

In this comparison we found that the two VRQ ranges 98-109 and 110-121 showed the most marked differences. This is indicated by the larger t test values which are associated with these columns of the table. In the lower of these two ranges, mixed ability prognoses were better than Stanbridge whereas in the higher range, these prognoses were lower. This result does seem to confirm the idea put forward in Section 3.5 that accurate prognosis is difficult in a mixed ability situation and seems also to indicate that the difficulties occur for the middle ability pupils.

Table 6.4 Comparison of the mean level of prognosis between the grouping system; in relation to VRQ.

Hall		VRQ RANGES					
		Below 73	74-85	86-97	98-109	110-121	Above 122
	Mean	1.60	1.75	2.77	3.10	4.51	4.59
St.	S.D.	0.81	0.85	1.17	1.34	1.08	1.19
	n	50	133	204	274	158	51
	Mean	1.29	2.00	2.57	3.57	4.19	4.58
B+W	S.D.	0.55	1.02	1.03	1.24	1.22	1.21
	n	24	213	438	475	357	198
B+W/S							
	F ratio	2.16	1.42	1.28	1.18	1.27	1.04
	t test	1.69	0.24	2.20	4.84	2.89	0.06

6.4 The Use of Prognoses in Counselling.

The aim of this section is to reveal any difference which may exist in the extent to which form teachers make use of prognosis information during the counselling process. We approached this by dividing the prognosis categories into two groups. The 'high prognosis' group consisted of categories 1, 2 and 3 and the 'low prognosis' group of the remaining categories 4-6. We then studied each pupil's subject choice and counted up to how many times a subject, actually chosen but having a low prognosis, could have been replaced by a subject which was not chosen but which had a high prognosis. (In the computer programme which was used this process was actually carried out by finding which was the smaller of the following numbers (i) the number of low prognosis subjects that were actually chosen by the pupils, and (ii) the number of good prognosis subjects that were not chosen.) The number of subjects which, on prognosis grounds *alone*, would have been more suitable for the pupil was then averaged over the individual hall populations. These results are shown in Table 6.5.

Table 6.5 Number of Better Subject Choices in each Hall . . . as Indicated by Prognosis Data

Hall	Mean No. of Better Choices	Standard Deviation	No. of Students
Br	1.20	0.9	98
Wy	1.10	0.9	102
St	1.21	0.9	92
Br+Wy	1.15	0.9	200

F ratio and t tests on these results reveal no significant differences between grouping systems, or between individual halls in the mixed ability system.

If one system had made greater use of prognosis than the other we would have expected that system to show a smaller number of 'better choices'. Since this is not the case we can find no evidence to suggest that counsellors in the two systems vary in the extent to which they use prognosis information.

To put the results of Table 6.5 rather more into perspective it is useful to call to mind that each pupil makes seven subject choices. Of these, on average, two were found to be supported by high prognoses (In Broughton and Wykham the mean number supported by good prognoses was 1.8, s.d.=2.2 n=200; in Stanbridge the mean was 2.0, s.d.=2.2 n=92; F and t tests again showed no difference between systems[1]).

Finally, in interpreting these figures one should remember that they were designed as a way of comparing prognosis in the two grouping systems within Banbury School and not as a means of testing the system of prognosis in general terms. For example one should keep in mind the fact that a far from negligible proportion of pupils (perhaps as high as 30%) will have no high prognoses for any subject and that they will, of necessity, reduce the mean number of subjects supported by good prognoses, however carefully the prognosis data has been used to guide their choices.

---

[1] s.d.=standard deviation.　　n=number of cases.

Pupil Attitudes

7.1 Introduction.

This chapter is intended as a very brief account of the survey which we carried out on pupil attitudes as most of the use to which this survey has been put has already been reported piecemeal in earlier chapters. The data has been used as background data in the analysis of other aspects of the project and this chapter merely adds extra information which can be obtained from the attitude study *per se*.

The main findings were:

(i) that pupils from a mixed ability background had better attitudes towards the school as a social community while attitudes to the school as a working community seemed not to be significantly affected by early grouping differences.

(ii) that this difference in attitude was particularly marked in the case of girls.

We found the selection of suitable tests for the assessment of attitudes at the age of sixteen quite difficult. Discussion at NFER led us to use two tests. One, which was the Amount of Social Interaction Instrument (ASI)[1], was intended to measure pupil participation and integration in the school as a social community. The other, the Subject Choice Satisfaction Scale, was a test designed to assess satisfaction with courses, and therefore to provide some insight into attitudes to the school as a working community. This second test is discussed in '*A Matter of Choice*' (M Reid *et al;* NFER). Appendix 12 in this report quotes the questions which were set to the pupils following with minor changes of wording which brought them in line with Banbury School terminology.

Additional scales were available from the ASI instrument but it was decided that they each correlate so highly with the scale which we did use (ASI Scale 1) that little additional information would be gained and at the same time the setting and marking problems would increase to an extent that would severely stretch the resources of the project. A table of these correlations, taken from 'A Matter of Choice' is included in Appendix 12.

Some additional information was derived by a simple study of pupils' absence. With the help of the Deputy Head of the Upper School persistent absentees were identified and the numbers from the individual halls were compared. It has been shown in many studies that absenteeism is a good indicator of poor attitude to school so this data provided an additional comparison between the attitudes of pupils from different halls.

All attitude measurements were made towards the end of the pupils' fifth year so they were able to assess genuine differences in attitude to the same Upper School, and not differences in attitude to their original hall bases.

7.2 ASI Scale 1 Student Participation and Integration.

The mean scores on this test were as follows:

Table 7.1 ASI Test Means for each Hall.

Hall	Mean	Standard Deviation
Broughton	46.3	7.0
Wykham	46.9	6.4
Stanbridge	44.1	6.4

[1] Finlayson D. S., Bank O., Loughram J. L., *op cit.*

These results compare with a mean of 41.4 (standard deviation=10.1) achieved in a study of 978 pupils in 14 comprehensive schools by Finlayson, *et al.*

We applied F and t tests to these results and quote the outcome below:

Table 7.2 ASI Comparisons between Halls and grouping systems.

Hall	F value	degrees of freedom	t value	degrees of freedom
Br + Wyk v Stanbridge	1.03 (NS)	122	72	2.688	194 Significant at 1% B+W have higher mean
Br v Wyk	1.32 (NS)	50	71	0.618	121 NS
B+W v S BOYS	1.52 (NS)	68	27	0.595	95 NS
B+W v S GIRLS	1.08 (NS)	44	53	2.815	97 Significant at 1% B+W have higher mean

It would appear that attitudes are rather more positive in Broughton and Wykham than in Stanbridge. This appears to be particularly so amongst the girls. All individual halls and the school as a whole had significantly higher scores than those found in the study of 14 schools mentioned above.

7.3 Subject Choice Satisfaction Scale (SCSS).

The mean values for this scale are quoted below.

Table 7.3 SCSS Test Means for each Hall.

Hall	Mean	Standard Deviation
Broughton	22.7	6.8
Wykham	24.9	6.1
Stanbridge	23.3	6.6

A full set of F and t tests were carried out on this data and no significant differences were found for boys, girls or all pupils. The tests compared systems, and halls within the mixed ability system.

No result were available on this test from other schools so we were unable to compare Banbury School with any sort of norm.

7.4 Relationship of the ASI and SCSS scales to other background data.

We calculated correlation coefficients for each hall between each of the new attitude scales and five other pieces of background information which we had already collected. The five other areas were :

    i) VRQ.

    ii) Socio Economic Group.

    iii) ABCFG—this is the mean score on the a,b,c,f, & g scales of the earlier attitude tests used by Phase One. The reason for grouping these particular scales together is discussed in Section 2.4.2 of this report—this group of scales assesses overall scholastic attitude.

    iv) HJ—the mean score on the h & j scales which assess anxiety in the classroom.

    v) DE—the mean score on the d & e scales which assess attitude to school class.

Table 7.4 shows the results of these calculations.

Table 7.4 Correlation of attitude scales with earlier background data

Hall	ASI	SCSS	ABCFG	HJ	DE	VRQ	SEG
Correlations with ASI scale							
B	1.0	.527*	−.415*	.526*	.271*	.202	.230*
W	1.0	.444*	.091	.037	−.031	−.101	.220*
B+W	1.0	.485*	−.112	.296*	.115	.030	.231*
S	1.0	.311*	−.072	.039	.153	.054	.010
Correlations with SCSS scale							
B	.527*	1.0	−.279*	.285*	.029	−.032	.106
W	.444*	1.0	−.092	−.072	.001	−.012	.167
B+W	.485*	1.0	−.132	.134	.028	.024	.127*
S	.311*	1.0	−.132	.359*	.161	.167	.276*

Significant coefficients are marked with an asterisk

The difference between these coefficients for Br+Wy and St were then checked for significance. For the SCSS Scale this was found in one case only. The correlation between HJ and SCSS was stronger in the streamed situation and the significance in the difference between correlations was 5%.

For the ASI scale one significant difference was also found. The correlation between ASI and HJ was stronger for pupils from the mixed ability situation, the significance of the difference being 5%. The correlation between ASI and Socio-Economic Group was also stronger for pupils from the mixed ability situation, the difference this time just failing to reach 5% significance.

The last result calls for some comment. It implies that a high ASI score (favourable attitude) is more likely to be linked to a high score on the Socio-Economic Group scale (ie. the basic manual end of the scale) if the pupil comes from the mixed ability system. We might suppose that the offspring of professional parents would have less favourable attitudes to the school if they found themselves to be in a mixed ability system. This could be a result of the suspicion with which such parents might regard the mixed ability situation (for this would tend to be different from the environment in which they gained their own education).

7.5 Persistent Absences.

We counted up, as persistent absentees, all pupils whose absences from school gave cause for concern, either as a result of their number, or for some other reason (such as inadequate explanation on a number of occasions, forged explanatory notes etc.). The numbers were divided up according to the hall from which the pupils had originated.

Table 7.5 Persistent Absentees.

Hall	No. Absenting Persistently	Total No. In Hall Group
B	13	76
W	0	87
S	10	91

The fluctuation between Broughton and Wykham is such that no evidence can be found here for differences between grouping systems.

Statistical techniques

8.1 Introduction.

The following notes are intended as a guide to the terms used in the text and the method of analysis used in the research. They are intended as reference for the reader who does not wish to go deeply into the mathematical theories but wishes to follow the methods and reasoning with some understanding.

The reader will quickly realise that results of many tests have been accumulated for analysis in the project and will also be aware of the dangers of trying to draw conclusions from such figures without mathematical justification. Statistics is a branch of mathematics in which the *valid* conclusions which can be drawn from a set of experimental results are often quite different from what ones intuition would have one believe.

The underlying mathematics to the various statistical procedures can be very deep though the procedures themselves are quite straightforward. The reader who has not studied the subject closely will have to accept that these mathematical justifications exist; it would be out of place to discuss them here as there are many texts which could be consulted at all levels. It must be said that this project would be merely a set of opinions and biased judgements without the use of statistical tests, and their results form the basis on which we make our conclusions (that is not, of course, to say that they draw our conclusions for us— we have to make our own judgements based on all available evidence).

The tests we have used are well known and, on the whole, simple to apply with straightforward interpretation.

For completeness and for the benefit of those readers not confident in their understanding of the subject we start with basic, yet key, ideas.

8.1.1 Summary of Items To Be Discussed

8.2 Some Basic Terms

8.2.1 Probability

This is a word with a loose everyday meaning but a precise mathematical meaning. The probability of something happening is given as a number between 0 and 1 which expresses how likely it is that the event will happen. A probability of 1 expresses certainty. A probability of 0 expresses impossibility. The convention in statistics is to use percentages rather than decimals or fractions eg. 10% probability means a probability of 0.1 or 1/10.

In any test or measurement there is a chance of error. An estimate of the probabilities of the possible errors could help us interpret measurements which were made. For example suppose we develop a test to be given to candidates in order to allocate them to sets for mathematics. We might calculate that there is a 0.1 (or 10%) probability that each individual is wrongly placed. This means that if the test is administered many times we would expect (about) one out of every ten to be misplaced. It would be a matter for our judgement if this was an acceptable probability.

The concept of probability as a measure of likelihood of an event happening is in itself quite simple, yet it is the basis of all that we do in statistics.

8.2.2 Probability Distribution

If we perform an experiment or make some measurement from a test there will be a set of possible results. Some results are more likely to be achieved than others and we can often calculate, by use of our knowledge and experience of the test, the probability of each of the possible outcomes. This we call the probability distribution. Clearly there are many distributions, there being many tests in many fields of study.

There are, however, many parallels and several commonly occuring distributions of probability. The names of these have no obvious meanings eg. F-distribution, which is named after Fisher, a statistician who demonstrated much of its background theory.

As an example, suppose we set a test in which the probability of an individual child, chosen at random, passing is $\frac{3}{4}$. Suppose there are 30 children in the chosen sample and we are interested in how many will pass. We can calculate the probability distribution for the nummer of passes

$$\text{probability of n passes} = \frac{n!}{30!\,(30-n)!} \times \left(\frac{3}{4}\right)^{n} \times \left(\frac{1}{4}\right)^{30-r}$$

$$\left[n! = 1.2.3.4.\,-\,-\,-\,-\,-\,-\,-\,\cdot\,(n-2)(n-1)\,n\right]$$

This is an example of the Binominal Distribution.

Though each distribution has its own formula for calculating the probabilities, we can often make use of standard tables in which they can be looked up. This obviously saves much time and hard work in carrying out the caluculations.

It is possible in the construction of tests to adjust the method of allocating marks to ensure that the numbers of people having each score follows a chosen distribution formula, so that the probability of any individual chosen at random (ie. nothing is known about him and the choice of him from the group is not contrived in any way) getting a particular score is according to the probability distribution used. For example, we have adjusted our VRQ ranges to fit a Normal Distribution.

For different values of μ and σ (see 8.2.5)—it can be shown that these are the mean and standard deviation of the distribution) the graph of

$$Y = \frac{1}{\sigma\sqrt{2\pi}}\ e^{-\frac{1}{2}(x-\mu)^2/\sigma^2} \qquad (e = 2.718)$$

gives one of the family of Normal curves and leads to a case of the Normal Probability Distribution. Two examples of the bell-shaped curves generated by this formula are given below.

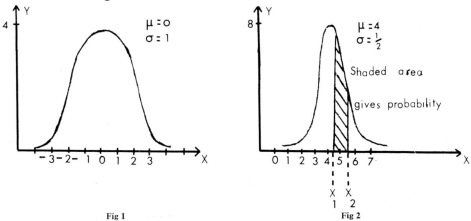

Fig 1   Fig 2

If the result of the test we are considering follows the Normal Distribution then the probability of its value lying between the values of x_1 and x_2 is the area under the graph between x_1 and x_2 (see fig. 2), whatever the values of x_1 and x_2 might be. Clearly the mathematics can be involved but the statistician can by-pass this by use of standard tables.

8.2.3 Population

In statistics, this can have a wider meaning than just a set of people. A population is a set of objects with some common quality. In our case we are in fact making measurements on people—pupils, from different teaching systems. These represent SAMPLES from some larger populations. Our measurements and statistical tests are to aid us in assessing whether these samples belong to the *same* population ie. the population with the particular quality that we are investigating. It is because of the deeper mathematical formulation of a problem that we talk in these terms. If, therefore we say that we are testing whether two samples are from the same population, we are merely checking to se if they score equally well (within reasonable bounds) on a particular test. For example we may wish to know if pupils from a mixed ability background differ in terms of VRQ from those in a streamed situation. The samples are the pupils that we study (ie. all those in the years group under investigation—the stamples are as large as possible). The population is described by the quality of VRQ that we are looking for in both systems (a normal distribution of scores over the pupils).

8.2.4 Statistic

This, quite simply, is a single number calculated from a set of results of a test on a sample. For example the statistic could be the average mark gained by pupils in an examination. There are many such statistics that we can use. With any set of results from which the statistic is to be calculated there are likely to be errors. Each candidate would have scored differently if tested on different occasions. If one applied a well tried test to the candidates one would have good estimates of the probabilities of each error occuring—the probability distribution of the error. This would in turn lead, via background calculations, to a probability distribution for the values of the chosen statistic.

The technique of statistics now becomes clear. We first subject our samples to a known and valid test from which we obtain a table of scores. We decide on a statistic, and calculate it from the scores for each sample. We aim to check if the two samples are from the same population. We check the probabilities of gettng these particular values for the statistic if they are from the same population, and hence assess if these probabilities are acceptable values for the assumption to be valid.

All we need are some techniques for doing this.

8.2.5 Mean, Variance, Standard Deviation

To help us to discuss the important general terms introduced in Sections 8.2.6 to 8.2.8 we here define three simple examples of a statistic. There are many statistics which we could use to form a judgement on a table of scores. The most widely known is the mean. This is one of the "averages" which we could examine and about which much is written

$$\text{The Mean Value} = \frac{\text{Total of all scores}}{\text{Total number of cases}}$$

We use the letter 'm' for the mean of a sample. It gives what can be taken as a representative value for the scores. It cannot give all possible information about the scores; it does not for example tell us how closely the individual scores approach the mean.

As a measure of whether there is a large or small spread of scores we invent another statistic. It is calculated as follows. First find the mean (m) for all scores and then find the difference between each score (x) and the mean. We square this quantity (the value obtained is therefore positive) and add the values so obtained. If we now divide by the number of scores (n) we obtain a second average: the mean of the squared differences between each score and the sample mean. This is the VARIANCE. The larger its value is, the wider is the spread of scores.

$$\text{Variance} = \frac{\sum (x - M)^2}{N}$$

Where m is the sample mean
x represents a score
n is the number of scores
Σ means "take the sum of all such expressions"

If we quote the mean and variance of a set of scores we are giving an idea of a typical score and the spread of scores in just two numbers. It is more usual, however, to quote the square root of the variance. Since we have taken the square of the quantity (x—m) for each score 'x', it makes sense to take a square root at the end so that in some way the result gives an idea of how far a typical score can be expected to be from the mean. The square root so found is called the STANDARD DEVIATION. We use the letter 's' for the standard deviation and s^2 for the variance of a sample.

$$s = \sqrt{\frac{\sum (x - M)^2}{N}}$$

The reader will appreciate that quoting m and s instead of perhaps hundreds of scores which cannot be analysed at a glance, can be a convenient summary. Clearly, however, these two statistics do not convey all the information possible about the scores; for example if two samples have the same mean and standard deviation, we cannot say that the samples have identical scores (for many obvious reasons), nor can we imply without further study that they are from the same population. However, we can use *these* statistics as a basis for *further* statistics and hence make inferences about the samples based on the underlying probability distributions.

8.2.6 Parametric and Non-Parametric Tests

A statistical test involves the calculation of a chosen statistic and the calculation (or looking up in tables) of the probability that the statistic could take that particular value based on a hypothesis about the samples (eg. that they are from the same population.) The probability thus found is then used as evidence to accept or reject the hypothesis. Certain tests rely for their validity on underlying probability distributions being of a certain kind. These are called Parametric Tests. For example, suppose we are testing to see if two samples come from the same population with respect to VRQ measurement. We know that the VRQ test gives a normal distribution of results. Background mathematical theory tells us that this will also imply that the difference in means of the two samples should follow a normal distribution. Calculation of this statistic and examination of the Normal probability tables then gives the probability that we should get this value for the statistic if the samples are in fact from the same population.

The analysis depends, however, on the background Normal distribution, so it is a parametric test.

There are many occasions when we cannot be confident about background distributions. Tests have been developed which are not dependent on this knowledge. They are called non-parametric or distribution-free tests (that is not to say that the chosen statistic is not linked to a distribution. It is just that we make no assumption about the probability distribution of the scores themselves). The t-test and F-test are examples of parametric tests; the underlying distributions are usually normal. The Chi-Squared (χ^2) and Gamma (γ) tests are examples of non-parametric tests.

8.2.7 Significance

This is a key word in our analysis. When we administer a statistical test, we are testing to see if two (or more) samples come from the same population, i.e. have some particular quality in common. For example, have pupils from mixed-ability background succeeded in mathematics more often than those from a streamed system when both sets started out with relevant qualities in common? To examine this we might assess the examination results of candidates from the two systems by use of one or more statistical tests. Rather like British Justice which sets out believing an accused person innocent until proved guilty, the common statistical tests are based on the assumption that the two samples are from the same population and this is only to be contradicted by a conclusion which makes this assumption absurd. The reader will feel that this is reasonable because the samples started out at a common level and were only subjected to different treatments. It would be a personal judgement on the systems if we started by believing the opposite assumption. The mathematics in some way reflects this.

When we have applied the statistical test, we have a measurement (for example the difference between the means of the samples). If we could then calculate the probability of this result occurring, based on the assumption that the samples did not differ on this quality in any real way, we could make a judgement as to whether the assumption is indeed correct. For example, suppose we obtained a difference of 11 in our sample means, and tables showed that there was only a probability of 2% (0.02) that such a result could be obtained if the two examples were from the same population (equally good at maths in our example), we would say that such a low probability was unacceptable and that this was good evidence for saying that the samples were indeed different in this quality. We would report our result as being SIGNIFICANT AT THE 2% LEVEL. Cearly the *LOWER* the percentage significance level, the more likely it is that the samples have a real difference—that the observed differences in scores are not just a result of chance.

More formally, the level of significance is the probability that we should get this value or more extreme values for the statistic we have used if the samples are from the same population.

When we are saying that a particular test gives a "significant difference", we are saying that the level of significance achieved is below the accepted level for assuming the samples to be from the same population.

The commonly accepted percentage probabilities used as evidence enough to reject the hypothesis of no difference is 5% or less. It is postulated that figures like 10% are too high. Even so, we must beware of spurious significance values. If we make many statistical comparisons based on a number of tests of our candidates, we increase the likelihood of our obtaining at least one low value of probability by chance alone. It would appear that the more we test our candidates, the greater is the chance of showing them to be different on at least one test. The statistician must be aware of this in his interpretation of results.

With each of the common statistical tests comes a table of values of significance, so that we can look up the result directly and avoid need to perform difficult calculations.

8.2.8 Degrees of Freedom.

Common statistical tests like the t-test and chi-squared test generate a family of background probability distributions. The particular distribution that we need is governed by the number of cases in the sample. These numbers have to be taken into account when the probabilities are calculated. The technique is to use the number of cases to find a number called the degrees of freedom. This new number is then used to identify the correct distribution curve (or, in practice, the correct part of the table) from which the probability associated with a given value of the statistic can be found. We will illustrate this idea by reference to the t-test. In this test we find the total number of cases (pupils, in our research) in the samples and subtract 2. This gives the number of degrees of freedom. (In fact this is the least number of scores that we would need to know if we knew the totals of all scores in each sample separately, and we wished to determine each individual score.) This tells us where to look in the t-test table, a sample of which is shown below.

Section of t test table.

DEGREES OF FREEDOM		VALUE OF P			
	—	.1	.05	.01	—
16	—	1.746	2.120	2.921	—
17		1.740	2.110	2.898	
18		1.734	2.101	2.878	
19		1.729	2.093	2.861	
20	—	1.725	2.086	2.845	—

This table gives the values of t which are exceeded with probability P.

Suppose we calculated the t statistc for, say, results on a mathematics test by pupils from two teaching systems (see Section 8.3.2) and were considering examples of sizes 9 and 11. The number of degrees of freedom would be $9+11-2=18$. Suppose the value of t turned out to be 2.34. By reference to the table, looking at the figures level with 18 in the degrees of freedom column, we find our result greater than the 0.05 level but less than the 0.01 level. We would report that the samples differed on the t-test with a signifiance about the 5% level. If 5% was our boundary for rejecting the hypothesis that the samples did not differ, we would have evidence to say that the systems differed on mathematical ability. An examination of the means of maths scores in the samples would indicate which gave the better results.

In situations other than the t-test the number of degrees of freedom can be found, though the procedures vary with the test being used.

Though the number of degrees of freedom have to be carefully considered in the construction of the statistical table probabilities, they are used by the experimenter only to locate the part of the table where he will find the relevant figures.

Statistical tables are published for the common tests and are straight-forward to use.

8.2.9 Covariance and Correlation

We are now in a position to introduce two more examples of useful statistics. Suppose we wish to establish whether VRQ and ability in mathematics are closely related. For each pupil in our sample we could plot a point on a scatter diagram. The horizontal axis could be VRQ and the vertical axis the score on a mathematics test. There are several sorts of resultant diagrams.

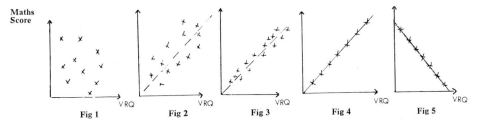

In Fig 1 the results are scattered in no recognisable pattern. In Fig 2 and more so in Fig 3 the results cluster about a straight line.

If the results were to lie on a straight line as in Fig 4, we could say that VRQ score and Mathematical score were closely related—the higher one is, the higher is the other. They vary together. If this were so we could use VRQ score to predict potential in mathematics. It would be useful to have a single statistic which would sum up how closely the two measurements varied together. The 'Covariance' is such a statistic.

This Covariance is calculated as follows. First calculate the means of the two scores to be tested (mean VRQ and mean score at maths in our example). Call these m_1 and m_2. Then for each possible score of the first kind, x_1, and the corresponding score of the second kind y_1 calculate $(x_1-m_1) \cdot (y_1-m_2)$. Add for all such values and divide by the number of cases, n, to reach the final result.

This process can be expressed in the formula

$$\text{Covariance} = \frac{\sum (x_i - m_i)(y_i - m_2)}{n}$$

A more useful statistic is found by dividing this by the product of the two standard deviations of the two sets of scores. This is the CORRELATION COEFFICIENT (p).

$$\rho = \frac{\sum (x_1 - M_1)(Y_1 - M_2)}{n\, S_1\, S_2}$$

A more convenient formula for direct calculation is

$$\rho = \frac{n\sum x_1 Y_1 - (\sum x_1).(\sum y_1)}{\sqrt{(n\sum x_1^2 - (\sum x_1)^2)(n\sum Y_1^2 - (\sum Y_1)^2)}}$$

$n =$ No of pairs of scores
$\sum x_1 y_1 =$ Sum of products of pairs of scores
$\sum x_1 =$ Sum of scores of one variable
$\sum y_1 =$ Sum of scores of other variable
$\sum x_1^2 =$ Sum of squared scores of one variable
$\sum y_1^2 =$ Sum of squared scores of other variable

The correlation coefficient is always a number between -1 and $+1$ inclusive. A value close to $+1$ indicates a strong "positive correlation"—as in Fig 4. A value close to 0 indicates no real correlation (Fig 1). Values close to -1 indicate a strong "negative correlation"—the scores do vary together but the higher one is the lower the other is (Fig 5). Clearly, if we are interested in what characteristics (eg. VRO, Differential Aptitudes, Attitudes) are needed in various aspects of schooling (eg. Performance in the different subjects studied), correlation coefficients will play a key role in the analysis.

8.3 The Tests Used in the Project.

8.3.1 Introduction.

A variety of tests of significance are available for the researcher, each with its particular aims and limitations. The skill lies in choosing the most appropriate one for the investigation to be conducted after examining what is available.

The aim is clear; to examine various tables of results, combine into a single statistic and find the probability of obtaining this value for the statistic—the significance—if our two samples were from the same population. We judge, from the level of significance if it is reasonable to reject or accept the hypothesis that the two samples have the quality under investigation in common (that is, are they from the same population?).

In our investigations we have considered, in general, comparisons between scores in the two teaching systems. Sometimes, however, we have studied results within systems in order to strengthen our conclusions on differences between systems. Our samples could consist of between one and two hundred cases, and, therefore, the use of a computer to facilitate calculations was necessary. Files of results were set up and programmes written to combine or sift out relevant data. Each calculation in itself was, in general, straightforward but when one is making selections based on a large number of factors such as Hall, Sex, Subject and background criteria such as VRQ or Differential Aptitude scores, one soon generates an enormous number of statistical tests (this has been of the order of 1000 or more on one computer run). The computer has been essential in order not only to get all the necessary results but to obtain accurate calculations.

76

In the formulae which are quoted in the following sections, the interpretation of symbols used, is as follows :

m_1 = The mean of the first group of scores
m_2 = The mean of the second group of scores
Σx_1^2 = The sum of the squared score values of the first group
Σy_1^2 = The sum of the squared score values for the second group
$(\Sigma x_1)^2$ = The square of the sum of the scores of the first group
$(\Sigma y_1)^2$ = The square of the sum of scores of the second group
n_1 = The number of scores in the first group
n_2 = The number of scores in the second group

8.3.2 The t-Test

If two samples have a significantly different mean, then we can say with confidence that they are not from the same population. The t statistic is used to examine such differences in means.

There is one complication in that the t-test that we normally use is only valid if the samples are drawn from populations with the same variance. We must, therefore, examine this before we proceed and we do so by means of the F-test (Section 8.3.3). This procedure is as follows; first test whether there is a significant difference in the variances of the populations (F-test). If there is then quote this significance as indicating that the samples are not from the same population. If there is not a significant difference in variances, then apply the t-test to see if there is a significant difference in means, which could again indicate that the samples are not from the same population. The reader will be aware of the possibility of samples coming from populations with no difference in means, yet having a difference in variance—a different statistic altogether—or vice versa. Indeed they may come from populations with similar means and variances but differ on some other statistic. Our conclusions from F and t tests only indicate differences in mean and variance. If no differences are shown we cannot be certain that the samples are from the same population. We have not produced enough evidence to reject the assumption, that is all. On the other hand a significant difference of 5% or less in general, can be taken as strong evidence that the assumption of no difference is not justified. We must always have in mind, however, what we mean by the samples differing in a particular quality. For example, we might say that our assessment of ability in maths of a sample is measured completely by the mean score of the sample, in which case the t-test is decisive for or against the assumption. The statistician must first of all decide what he is setting out to assess before deciding what test he is to use.

The formula for the t statistic is

$$t = \frac{M_1 - M_2}{\sqrt{\left(\dfrac{\Sigma x_1^2 - (\Sigma x_1)^2}{n_1} + \dfrac{\Sigma y_1^2 - (\Sigma y_1)^2}{n_2} \right) \left(\dfrac{1}{n_1} + \dfrac{1}{n_2} \right)}}$$

The number of degrees of freedom is $(n_1 + n_2 - 2)$.

Standard tables for the t statistic significances are available.

If we are only interested in a difference in means, or cannot assume that the variances are the same, we by-pass the F-test but cannot use the above formula for t. Instead we use

77

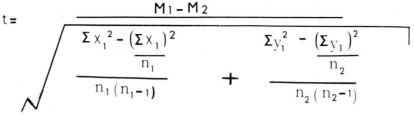

$$t = \cfrac{M_1 - M_2}{\sqrt{\cfrac{\Sigma x_1^2 - (\Sigma x_1)^2}{n_1 (n_1 - 1)} + \cfrac{\Sigma y_1^2 - (\Sigma y_1)^2}{n_2 (n_2 - 1)}}}$$

This can only be used if n_1 and n_2 are large ($N > 30$)

The underlying population is assumed to be Normally Distributed for the t-test. Small deviations can be shown to be still valid, and also the use of large samples enable deeper theories of probability to show that the t-test is valid.

8.3.3 The F-test

As explained in 8.3.2 we have used this to examine whether or not we can make the assumption that our samples come from populations with the same variance, as this is a necssary condition to make the t-test valid. The technique is based on the fact that one can make an estimate of the variance of the *population* (σ^2) from the data on a *sample* from that population. For a sample of size n, the estimated population variance is given by:

$$\sigma^2 = \frac{\left(\Sigma x^2 - \cfrac{(\Sigma x)^2}{n} \right)}{(n - 1)}$$

For the F-test two such estimates σ_1^2 and σ_2^2 are made from the two samples. The F statistic is then calculated as

$$F = \frac{\sigma_1^2}{\sigma_2^2}$$

where σ_1^2 is taken as the larger variance.

The number of degrees of freedom are given by two numbers $(n_1 - 1)$ and $(n_2 - 1)$. If the samples come from the same population, σ_1^2 will be approximately equal to σ_2^2 and F will be near to 1. The further F is from unity, the bigger the probability that the samples come from different populations.

Once F is known, standard F distribution tables are consulted for the measure of significance. Our method of σ_1^2 being the larger variance requires us to double the probabilities from the standard tables.

8.3.4 Analysis of Variance

When we have a large number of groups between which comparisons can be made by using, for example a t-test (eg. in the 21 possible comparisons between pairs of the following halls, B, W, S, D, B+W, S+D, B+W+S+D) we increase (by a factor of 21 in the example given) our chance that a statistically significant result will appear as a result of chance alone. A more appropriate technique than multiple t-tests in this situation, is Analysis of Variance. In our study we have, in general, only been comparing two systems or two halls within one system. The pairs of halls whose results were to be compared were therefore decided in advance by the very nature of the project. We have only rarely been making multiple t-test comparisons of the kind discussed above, and so Analysis of Variance has rarely been necessary.

On the occasions where multiple t-tests have been used they have shown no significant differences. Since Analysis of Variance helps us to avoid spurious significances, its use would have added ltttle to our particular analysis.

8.3.5 Contingency Tables

If we can divide observations into several classes, based on a background criterion, we can count how many observations fall into each class for each system that we are studying. If we set the results out as a table, we call it a contingency table. For example, Table 4.2 in Chapter 4 gives a contingency table for O-level results.

Hall	1&2	3	4	5&6
B+W	123	109	51	96
S+D	104	110	54	127

A study of this table can lead to a conclusion about differences between the systems.

In our study we have frequently been able to partition results into class ranges; for example, Low (85 or less), Middle (85—110) and High (110 and above) VRQ. We have then counted up the numbers in each of the ranges. The table below shows the numbers choosing one science subject in year 4.

	Low VRQ	Mid VRQ	High VRQ
Streamed	17	48	10
Mixed Ability	25	26	1

If we can arrange results meaningfully like this, we can make use of non-parametric tests (tests which make no assumptions about the underlying distributions). There is an advantage in this, in that if differences are found by the statistical test, an examination of the table will show more clearly where the differences lie than is possible when tests such as the t-test are used. The number of rows and columns of the table can be any value theoretically. The number of degrees of freedom is (No. of Rows—1) x (No. of Columns—1).

8.3.6 Chi-Squared (χ^2) Test

The chi-squared method sets up a table similar to the contingency table which contains the expected numbers in the cells if there was no real difference between the samples. If the numbers in the cells of this expected table are greater than 5 (or better, 10) we can use the chi-squared statistic to examine whether there is a real difference between the samples. For example :

OBSERVED CSE GRADES (Actual Values)

Grades	1&2	3	4	5&6
B+W	117	238	223	124
S+D	223	239	254	200

EXPECTED RESULTS (Calculated from the above numbers if no real difference exists)

Grades	1&2	3	4	5&6
B+W	181.6	216.6	216.6	147.1
S+D	218.4	210.4	260.4	176.9

The reader will appreciate how difficult it would be to draw a valid conclusion by scanning the table by eye.

The expected numbers are found as follows for each cell.
(1)   Find the sum S of all the numbers in the table.
(2)   Find the sum R of all the numbers in the row in which the cell falls.
(3)   Find the sum C of all the numbers in the column in which the cell appears.

The expected number for that cell is then $(R \times C)/S$.

This ensures that row and column totals in the Expected table are the same as for the observed table. If we now find, in turn, the difference O—E between the observed and expected values in the corresponding cells of the tables, square the answer and divide by E, the expected value, we calculate the χ^2 statistic by adding all such values.

$$\chi^2 = \sum \frac{(O-E)^2}{E}$$

We then refer to a published table with this value and the number of degrees of freedom to obtain the significance level. (In the above example $\chi^2=11.1$ and there are 3 degrees of freedom. We find a significance of 2% or .02 from the table).

In the chi-squared test we are usually testing the hypothesis that there *is* a difference between the systems, and the table then gives us the probability that the difference is real (we would have obtained a result of 98%, or .98, in our example from the table). When the test is used in this way it is usual to subtract the table result from 1, in order to quote the significance level. In our example we arrived at a 2% significance level. This is interpreted as meaning that there was a low probability that we would obtain our observed results *if* there were *no* difference between the samples.

Study of the Observed and Expected tables show us where the differences lie. For example, B+W has lower numbers obtaining grades 1 & 2 at CSE and higher numbers obtaining grade 3 than would be expected if the systems did not differ.

8.3.7 The Gamma (γ) Test[1]

If we desire to measure the association between two variables whose classes can be ordered, we can use the Gamma statistic for analysis of the contingency table values, where one variable gives the row classification, and the other gives the column classification. Numbers in the cells need have no lower limit. For example, since prognosis and examination results are both ordered variables, we have used the Gamma test to measure for the degree of association between them in each grouping system.

The hypothesis tested by gamma is that the two variables are independent for the sample. Low percentage significance levels (5% or 1%) imply that there is a small chance that this hypothesis is correct and therefore imply significant levels of association. Low significance levels are linked to large values of gamma. A brief introduction to the methods of the test is given below. If there were an

---

[1] See *J. Am. Stat. Assoc.* Dec. 54 and June 63.

association between two variables we would expect that the higher the value of one variable, the higher would be the value of the other (grade and prognosis in our example). The idea behind the Gamma test is to calculate a statistic based on this. We imagine choosing two students at random from the sample. Based on the figures which appear in the contingency table we can calculate three probabilities for these two random choices. For simplicity of explanation we use the variables grade and prognosis as above. The work is the same for other suitable (ordered) variables.

P1=Probability that *either,* both grade and prognosis of first pupil is less than those of the second, *or,* that grade and prognosis of the first are both greater than those of the second.

P2=Probability that for one pupil, one of grade and prognosis is less, and the other is greater, than the corresponding grade and prognosis for the second pupil.

P3=Probability that both grade and prognosis of first pupil are equal to grade and prognosis for second.

If there is a strong association between grade and prognosis P1 will be large (approaching $+1$) and P2 will be small (approaching zero). P1-P2 could be used to assess the degree of association. In fact a better formula is

$$\frac{P1-P2}{1-P3}$$ and this is the statistic Gamma.

The higher the value of γ the higher is the association. The maximum value is 1. The closer the value is to zero the less is the association. We can have a negative value for γ, which means that there is negative association (the higher one variable the lower the other). The minimum value is -1. If all the numbers in the table were zero except those in the cells making the diagonal from top left to bottom right, $\gamma=1$. If all numbers in the cells were zero except those in the diagonal from bottom left to top right, $\gamma=-1$.

A further calculation, based on the probability distribution of Gamma, gives the significance levels for the calculated value of the statistic.

Comparison of degrees of association found for different systems will reveal differences between the systems based on these variables.

8.3.8 Fisher Exact Probability Test[1]

In cases where numbers are too small for chi-squared, and our results give a 2 x 2 contingency table, we can still obtain a significance level by the use of the Fisher Exact Probability Test. We obtain the probability that differences shown in the table, and more extreme cases, occur by chance.

Suppose that, in one of our subject analyses, the contingency table was as shown below.

Numbers Choosing Music.

	No. choosing	No. not choosing	Total
Streamed	A	B	A+B
Mixed Ability	C	D	C+D
Total	A+C	B+D	A+B+C+D

Let A+B+C+D=N.

---

[1] We are indebted to Mr. J. K. Backhouse for the use of his programs to calculate Gamma and Fisher probabilities, as no tables exist.

The probability of getting the given cell values when the row and column totals are fixed is

$$\frac{(A+B)!\ (C+D)!\ (A+C)!\ (B+D)!}{A!\ B!\ C!\ D!\ N!}$$

$$(N!=1.2.3.4\ldots(N-2)\cdot(N-1)N)$$

For the significance level we calculate this probability and the probability of 'more extreme' cell values when row and column totals are to remain fixed. Adding these gives the significance level. If the smallest number in our original table was S then S+1 calculations of probability would be needed.

For example, if in our original table A, B, C and D corresponded to the numbers 4, 5, 9 and 7 as shown,

A	B
C	D

4	5
9	7

the significance level would be the sum probabilities of each of the following tables. Each probability is calculated as shown above.

4	5		3	6		2	7		1	8		0	9
9	7		10	6		11	5		12	4		13	3

"this case"   <———   more extreme cases   ———>

8.3.9 Choice of Method When Cell Numbers Are Small

If cell numbers are too small for Chi-squared tests to be reliable, and if the table is not 2×2 (Fisher not appropriate), or if the variables are not ordered (Gamma not appropriate), we must decide if meaningful results can be obtained by combining classes.

For example, we might obtain the following table for numbers choosing (say) Art at CSE.

VRQ Range		1	2	3	4	5
System	B+W	3	5	12	6	4
	S+D	4	7	16	2	5

We have several cells with numbers below 5 and most are below 10.
By combining VRQ ranges 1 & 2 (as LOW VRQ) and ranges 4 & 5 (as HIGH VRQ) we can still apply the Chi-squared test meaningfully by studying

VRQ		LOW	MED	HIGH
System	B+W	8	12	10
	S+D	11	16	7

This course of action should be compared with a study of difference in means by the t-test, or with other possibilities available.

8.3.10 Significance of The Correlation Coefficient

When we calculate a correlation coefficient, p, between two variables (eg. VRQ and success in a maths exam), we wish to know if the value that we obtain can

82

be taken as indicating a real association between the variables or not. We could ask ourselves the question—what is the probability that we would achieve this value for the correlation coefficient if there was no correlation between the variables (viewing our results as being those for a sample from a population). If n is the number of cases in our sample, it can be shown that the statistic

$$\frac{\rho \sqrt{n-2}}{\sqrt{1-\rho^2}}$$

follows the t distribution with (n—2)degrees of freedom. This simple calculation and the use of the t tables will, therefore, produce a value for the significance of the correlation coefficient.

8.3.11 Regression Analysis

If we are interested in a particular measurement (eg. success of candidates in various examinations), we can often postulate what factors might contribute to high scores on that measurement (eg. various differential aptitudes, VRQ, attitudes to school). We could calculate the correlation coefficient between each of the factors and the variable being studied, and have some idea of which indeed were linked to it. There are also, however, the inter-correlations between these various factors to be considered. The study becomes quite complicated when many possible factors are present.

Regression analysis affords the opportunity to make clearer judgements than the examination of raw correlations allows. The study is deep and we can only give a few basic ideas here. We have made use of a standard programme from the SPSS package for our analysis. The information required for input is the correlation matrix, number of cases (students), means and standard deviations. Our main interests have been in analysing factors which could predict success in examinations. We also did similar preliminary work on factors correlating with choice of particular subjects by students in year 4. The subject choice, to some extent, being the result of counselling procedures could then be judged against results. If the factors which were linked to success were not those which led to choice, then a careful study of counselling procedures would be shown to be necessary.

If we can pick the appropriate factors which correlate with success, say, in maths, the programme would give us a prediction equation for this—that is, an equation that could be used to calculate, within bounds, the predicted result for a particular candidate when scores on other tests are known.

For example, suppose the analysis showed that the relevant differential aptitude scores to predict success in mathematics were SR (Space Relations), NA (Numerical Ability) and MR (Mechanical Reasoning), we would obtain a prediction equation such as

RESULT=.05×SR score +.026×NA score +.015×MR score +.54

If we then measured a candidate in year 4 on these differential aptitude tests, he might score 20 on SR, 30 on NA, 25 on MR.
The calculation would give

RESULT=2.945—a result at level 3
(level 1=failure, level 2=Grade 5, level 3=Grade 4 etc.).

Hence counselling could be facilitated at this early age if the predictor was reliable. Clearly the statistician should proceed with caution with statistics of this kind, but a usefulness is easily seen. One drawback is the difficulty in finding all contributory factors. An indication of how successful we have been comes with the output of the programme. This is termed the percentage variance. Figures below 100% indicate that some predictors have not been included in the correlation matrix. The Standard Error is another figure given. The result from the prediction equation can be judged as accurate within the limits set by the standard error. For example, if the standard error were .8 in our example, the value of the predicted grade would lie btween 2.145 and 3.745. A small standard error and a high proportion of variance indicate a reliable prediction equation.

The numbers to be used in our equation (.052, .026, .015 in our example) are called the 'b-values'. The number to be added at the end of the equation (.54 in our example) is called the Constant.

Since different tests have different scoring scales (eg. NA may score a maximum of 80, while SR scores a maximum of 45), we cannot assess the relative importance of the factors by comparing the b-values. The program calculates a second set of numbers, the beta (β) values or normalised b values, which can be compared to find the relative importance of the factors.

The regression equation is obtained step by step, a new variable entering the equation at each step, starting with the single best predictor. At each step the F-test is applied to see if the b-value of the next variable in the equation makes a significant different to the prediction equation. If the F value is too low it will not be included and calculation ceases. A deeper study of this method is recommended, firstly from the SPSS Handbook.

General Comments

9.1 Relationship of findings to the original research questions

It is not our intention in this chapter to collect together all of the detailed conclusions which have been stated in the introductions to each of the earlier chapters. We wish merely to bring general trends to the attention of the reader, and to relate these trends to the three questions to which we were asked to address ourselves. We will take each of the questions in turn in the three paragraphs which follow.

   (i)   Do the specific effects of mixed ability grouping, that were disclosed by Phase One of the research, continue beyond the point at which the pupils involved are working predominantly in a mixed ability situation?

We would suggest that there is much evidence in what has been presented in earlier chapters, to support the view that differences between the systems of grouping employed in the first years of a pupil's secondary schooling, can have long term effects on his secondary school career. The particular findings of Phase One (which were concerned with attitudes, attainment and friendship patterns) can all be recognised in similar findings relating to these areas, in the work of this study.

These differences between systems were usually associated with a lack of difference between the individual halls which make up the two systems. While this cannot be said to prove that the differences are a result of the grouping systems themselves, it does, at least, do nothing to disprove such a hypothesis.

   (ii)   Are there differences between the types of choice made by pupils from the two grouping backgrounds?

Very distinct differences in subject choice were discovered at fourth year level. These were supported by an independent study of Drayton School subject choice. Vestiges of these differences were found in sixth form subject choice. There seemed to be little doubt that grouping systems could affect these kinds of decision made by pupils. Career choice and aspiration for sixth form or technical college education after the age of 16, seemed to be matters which were not greatly dependent on early grouping system.

   (iii)   Are there differences in the ways in which pupils are advised by their counsellors and form teachers if they are taught in different grouping system?

There was some evidence to suggest that it was harder to assess the abilities (both those indicated by VRQ and those measured by CSE and O-level results examinations) of pupils in mixed ability groups. If these difficulties led to problems in subject choice counselling, they did not result in any lowering of pupils' satisfaction with courses or of the levels of overall performance in public examinations. The suggestion that counselling for subject choice would be done on a less individual basis in the streamed system (where pupils may be guided towards or away from 'hard' subjects largely on the basis of their allocation to high or low ability streams) was investigated and no evidence to support it was found. Since an investigation of the actual counselling *process* was outside the resources of this project this result is based on the study (described in Section 3.4.3.3ii) of the outcome of that process. This is clearly a less satisfactory methodology than one which looks closely at the process itself, and we suggest that such a study might usefully be carried out to investigate this matter more fully.

Most of the differences outlined above were sex dependent and many were dependent on the VRQs of the students involved.

Since several of the findings were in favour of the mixed ability system we should perhaps point out that they relate to pupils who passed through their mixed ability stage at a time when the whole exercise of mixed ability teaching at Banbury was in its infancy. Some questions could be raised as to whether the advantages would still exist when the enthusiasm surrounding a new venture had begun to wane and when the support and concern which were lavished on the preparations for the early years of the exercise, were no longer in evidence. Alternatively one might argue that advantages for this system which were in evidence at this early stage should surely be enhanced as experience and expertise in the new ways developed. Only a far longer enquiry could hope to approach such issues with any hope of success.

Some readers may have a sense of surprise that the existence of mixed ability groupings for such a short time in the educational career of pupils could have such large effects as those discussed in this report. In considering this point we should bear in mind that primary schools almost invariably adopt mixed ability groupings which the Barker Lunn[1] study has shown to have effects on the outcome of the primary stage. What we are comparing therefore, is a situation in which this arrangement, familiar to the pupils, is continued into the secondary phase, (to be replaced uneventfully and gradually by the introduction of streaming and setting in later years), and a situation in which there is a sudden and dramatic change to streaming at the moment of transfer to the secondary school. Seen in these terms, the existence of mixed ability groupings in the early secondary years is, from the pupils' point of view, a very different situation from that of streaming in year one. The long term effects of this organisational difference are not therefore at all surprising.

9.2 General Relevance of the Findings

The detailed findings of the study are, of course, presented elsewhere and each reader will select different areas as being of special importance to his own interests and needs. Here, however, we would like to suggest that the overall importance of this study is that it provides a general statistical overview of the long-term effects of mixed ability teaching in the first two years of a pupil's secondary school career. It can therefore provide a general insight into the differences which might be expected between the *outcomes* of the educational process in the two systems. It does not, except in a tentative and speculative way, offer any detailed explanations of the mechanisms by which such differences arise. Any attempt to provide such explanations must involve careful study of actual teaching styles, and procedures within the teaching and pastoral groups of schools. The present project may enable researchers who are able to undertake such detailed studies to plan their experiments with greater ease and higher chance of success, for it will acquaint them with areas which should be considered worthy of further investigation.

We would like to suggest that this study can also go some way towards freeing discussions on the topic of mixed ability teaching from the limiting effects of personal bias and unsubstantiated opinion. There is little here that will force the outcome of such discussions, but we feel that there is much which will stimulate and inform.

In both of the roles outlined above, the limitations of the project which arise from the structure of the Banbury situation and the timing of the two phases of the research will have to be borne in mind. They are set out in full in Chapter 1. Equally important, the strengths of the Banbury Project design (with

---

[1] Barker Lunn, Streaming in the Secondary Primary School, NFER 1970.

its opportunities for cross-checking within grouping systems, and its study of two systems which are closely matched, both with respect to the aims for which they are working and with respect to the ability levels and social backgrounds of the students who made up the two groups) should be remembered. These too are described in detail in Chapter 1.

9.3 Pointers for Future Study

Detailed indication of things which might be done to follow up individual results of this enquiry are to be found in the text. Again, in keeping with the style of this final chapter, we are here concerned with the more general issues which have arisen and which we feel are indicative of a need for larger scale follow up work.

(i) We were able to show that the level of success achieved in the prediction of student performance was lower than teachers might hope. This was especially so in the mixed ability situation but also applied to streamed groups. We were also able to show some pointers towards an alternative approach (Appendix 5) to this problem. We suggest that there is considerable need for further work in this important and always difficult area, and feel that a successful conclusion of such work would be of benefit to all schools, whether they adopt mixed ability systems or not.

(ii) The implications of the work on examination results (which suggested that the most and least able pupils may do slightly better from the mixed ability situation) could be regarded as very far reaching and should surely be followed up, especially in terms of the effects on the *very* able and *very* disadvantaged students.

In such a study of the "extremes", the concept of achievement could, with considerable benefit, be widened beyond that of achievement in public examinations. Some indications of the areas which might be included have already been given in Section 4.7.

In connection with achievement, further study of those students who formed mixed VRQ friendships is of particular interest, for it might be postulated that this potential social advantage of the mixed ability system is also a potential academic disadvantage for the most able students. (One might suppose that the high VRQ pupils with low VRQ friends may under-perform). We made a very tentative approach to this subject in our work but the results were so dependent on the personalities of the very small number of pupils involved that nothing of importance could be deduced. Work of this kind could fall naturally into any study of "the extremes".

A worthwhile study of these exceptional pupils could only be carried out across a large number of schools, for the number of such pupils in any one school is always small.

We suggest that the present project, in so far as it has shown that grouping systems can affect the examination performance of able and weak pupils, offers strong indications that the considerable investment required by a study of the extremes, would be handsomely rewarded.

(iii) Finally one might suggest that the 'single school' limitation of the Banbury study is one which should be overcome by the extension of the data base to include a larger number of schools. This would inevitably be a large scale exercise but it may well be worthwhile in view of the important implications of some of the results reported here (for example in the areas of subject choice and examination results).

9.4 Research Style

This is perhaps an unusual section to include in a research report. However, the structure of the research was sufficiently unusual that it would be wrong to say nothing about the difficulties inherent in this approach and, especially, about the advantages and opportunities that it offers.

First, one should remember that the research was carried out by two members of staff at Banbury School who were, during the period of the work, still heavily committed to teaching and to other duties which teaching posts have associated with them. The time available for the research was therefore approximately equal to six tenths of one man's time.

The pre-requisites, if such an arrangement is to be successful, are numerous. First there should be, readily to hand, expert guidance on technical matters. In this respect the Banbury Project was admirably served by Mr. J. K. Backhouse of the Department of Educational Studies at Oxford University. Secondly, the researchers need direct access to a university library and, if statistical procedures are involved, to a computer. This implies that the school in which the work is done cannot be too far from the university which is guiding the project. In our case the 23 miles separating Banbury and Oxford were often a considerable nuisance. We do not feel that a project could run smoothly over distances which were much greater than this. Thirdly, considerable care in the construction of the researchers' timetables is needed prior to the beginning of the research. Numerous blocks of time scattered through the week are no substitute for one whole day on which little or no teaching is done. Fourthly, the sympathetic understanding of colleagues within the school is essential, as is the full support and involvement of the head teachers in any school which is included in the study. (We are pleased to record that, in these respects we were extremely fortunate in the Banbury Project). Lastly, we feel that it is important that members of the school staff, in addition to the head, are involved in the overall control of the project through, as in our situation, a general Steering Group. In this way the requirements of the research are widely understood in the school and the results can more quickly be fed back into the consciousness of the whole body of staff. In addition, insight into the meaning and interpretation of findings is readily available to the researchers. Such a style of research necessarily implies a co-operative exercise; the inclusion of teaching staff on the Steering Group is the formal way in which this co-operation can be encouraged.

In view of this long, and perhaps costly list of pre-requisites, one might feel justified in supporting this kind of research style only if it offers considerable advantages over the more usual kinds of structure. We feel that it does so, and give below some of the advantages which were apparent to us while the research was in progress.

A major consideration is that it is possible to involve the school very closely in the work which is going on in connection with it. The staff can contribute to the planning stages, can be involved in the collection of data and can request extensions of analyses, or of the kinds of data collected, to help them with their own tasks within the school. All of these aspects were apparent in the Banbury Project. It is our opinion that a project beginning *de novo* in this style (rather than one which sets about to extend an earlier piece of work as did this project) might more easily exploit these advantages. It was particularly true in our case that there was little opportunity for the staff to be involved in the planning of the methodology, for, by nature of the fact that we were asked to follow up the findings of the first phase of the Banbury Enquiry, this methodology was already established to a considerable extent. We feel that genuine involvement at this planning stage is perhaps the best guarantee that a project can have of effective staff involvement through all of the later stages. It is probably true that there is nothing in this paragraph which is, of necessity, impossible in the context of a more normal research structure. Nevertheless, genuine school involvement is not easy to establish when teachers are so very busy with the day to day business of teaching, and it is strongly our opinion that a school-based project is far more likely to engage this involvement than is an apparently remote researcher who is injected into the school organism and who therefore runs the risk of being rejected by it.

If we accept that staff involvement is a consequence of this research style we might ask why such involvement is thought to be an advantage. First, we feel that it is bound to be of advantage to the research. An involved staff will the more readily participate when data is to be collected. They will more readily suggest explanations for results, perhaps enabling the researchers to probe more deeply, perhaps alerting them to spurious effects. Secondly, staff involvement can be of great benefit to the school. A research programme inevitably puts the school under an unusually close scrutiny. The "spin-off" from this can be a valuable increase in the understanding of the ways in which the school functions. Such a "spin-off" is probably only felt by the school if there is close involvement in the research for many of the useful snippits of information are of the kind which will never see publication in the final report.

Secondly, a major aspect of school-based research is the element of in-service training which it involves. The researchers themselves are, of course, especially privileged in this respect. Yet the in-service training is not restricted to them. We feel that, as a result of staffroom discussions and more detailed sessions with particularly interested staff, there has been a heightening of overall awareness of, for example, the potential and limitations of statistical methods. Inevitably some staff have shown more interest in this aspect than others but we feel that, when the report is published and the results can be seen as a whole, this aspect of in-service training will become even more apparent.

Lastly we would suggest that the school-based project gains from the fact that the researchers are actively involved in the activities of the school which they are studying. They are perhaps more aware of variables which might be important and of long term changes which have been taking place and which might underlie apparently established procedures within the school. Again they might be more alert to the impact of a testing programme on both the staff and the pupils and therefore might more easily avoid alienating either group by too much testing. Above all, they will be more aware of the potential, as research data, of information regularly assembled by the school as part of its normal administrative and academic procedures. In this way the amount of additional testing might be reduced (with obvious advantages to the students under study) but particularly, if data of this kind *is* used, staff (especially in that school, but also, we suspect, elsewhere) will be able to interpret it, and the results which are drawn from it as they are aware of its strengths and its limitations in a way that would rarely apply to data collected by unfamiliar objective tests.

There may of course be some situations in which a more remote researcher would be at an advantage (eg. if a great deal of classroom observation was involved or if comparisons between staff were part of the study) but we think that there is enough indication in what has been said in this section that the school-based approach to educational research is one which should be encouraged.

Finally, we would like to emphasise that this last section is very much a matter of opinion and that it lacks the objective basis which we hope to be a feature of the rest of this report.

BIBLIOGRAPHY

Anderson H., Hipkin J. and Plaskow M. (eds) — *Education for the Seventies* — Heinemann Educational Books 1970

Backhouse J. K. — *Statistics: An Introduction to Tests of Significance* — Longman 1967

Barker Lunn J. C. — *Streaming in the Primary School* — NFER 1970

Bennett G. K., Seashore H. G., & Wesman A. G. — *Fifth Manual for the Differential Aptitude Tests* — The Psychological Corporation 1974

Bradley J. and Meredith C. — *The Relationship of Early Preferences to Sixth Form Choice* — *J. of Applied Educational Studies* 4(2), 55-67

Brining J. L. & King J. L. — *Computational Handbook of Statistics* — Scott Foresman & Co. 1968

Child D. — *The Essentials of Factor Analysis* — Holt 1970

Craft M. (ed) — *Family, Class and Education A Reader* — Longman 1970

Craft M., Raynor J. & Cohen L. — *Linking Home and School* — Longman 1967

Davis R. — *The Grammar School* — Penguin 1967

Davies R. P. — *Mixed Ability Grouping* — Temple Smaith 1975

Droege R. C. — *Sex Differences in Aptitude Maturation During High School* — *J. Counselling Psych.* 1967 14, 407-11

Douglas J. W. B. — *The Home and the School* — MacGraw Hill 1964

Erricker B. C. — *Advanced General Statistics* — E.U.P. 1971

Evans K. M. — *Planning Small Scale Research* — NFER 1968

Flanagan J. C. et al — *Counsellors Technical Manual for Interpreting Test Scores (Project Talent)* — Palo Alto Calif 1961

Goodman L. A. & Kruskal W. H. — *Measure of Association for Cross Classification (Gamma)* — *J. American Stat. Ass.* 1954 1963

Holt J. — *How Children Fail* — Penguin 1969

Hutchings D., Bradley J. & Meredith C. — *Free to Choose—Origins and Prediction of Academic Specialisation* — Oxford University Dept. of Educational Studies

Hutchinson M. and Young C. — *Educating the Intelligent* — Penguin 1962

Jackson B.	Streaming—An Educational System in Miniature	R + K.P. 1964
Jackson and Marsden	Education and the Working Class	R + K.P. 1962
King R.	School Organisation and Pupil Involvement	R + K.P. 1973
Maccoby E. E. and Jacklin C. N.	The Psychology of Sex Differences	OUP 1975
Nash S. C.	Conceptions and Concomitants of Sex Role Stereotyping	Columbia Univ. 1973
Newbold D.	Ability Grouping—the Banbury Enquiry	NFER 1977
Nie, Bent and Hull	Statistical Package for the Social Sciences	McGraw Hill 1970
Parker R. E.	Introducing Statistics for Biology	E. A. Arnold 1973
Reid M. I., Burnett B. R. and Rosenburg H. A.	A Matter of Choice—A study of guidance and subject options	NFER 1974
Ross, Bunton Evison and Robertson	A Critical Appraisal of Comprehensive Education	NFER 1972
Seigal S.	Nonparametric Statistics	McGraw Hill 1966
Stott D. H.	The Social Adjustment of Children	ULP 1963
Wiseman S. and Pigeon D. A.	Curriculum Evaluation	NFER 1970

Appendices

An outline of the Banbury School Curriculum 1973-1974 Years 1 & 2

Table A1.1 shows the year 1 and year 2 curricula for Banbury School in the academic year 1973/74. At this time Cohort 3 was in year 2 and Cohort 4 in year 1. The table therefore gives a clear impression of the lower school curriculum as it affected the pupils who have been the subject of this study.

The curriculum was applied across all halls (including Drayton which was at that time still a hall of Banbury School). The week was divided into 35 forty minute periods.

Table A1.1 Banbury School Curriculum 1973-74 Years 1 & 2

SUBJECT	NUMBER OF PERIODS	
	YEAR 1 (C4)	YEAR 2 (C3)
ENGLISH SUBJECT GROUP		
English	6	5
Library	1	–
MATHEMATICS SUBJECT GROUP	5	5
HUMAN STUDIES SUBJECT GROUP		
Combined Studies	6	–
History	–	2
Geography	–	3
R.E.	–	2
SCIENTIFIC STUDIES GROUP		
Biology	2	2
Physical Science	–	4
LINGUISTIC STUDIES GROUP		
French	6	5
Other	-	-
DESIGN STUDIES GROUP		
Combined Craft	2	-
Art	2	3
Domestic Science	-	3 Girls
Technical Studies	-	3 Boys
Needlework	-	-
MUSIC	2	2
PHYSICAL EDUCATION		
Gymnastics	{ 2 Boys / 1 Girls	2 Boys / 1 Girls
Dance	1 Girls	1 Girls
Games	2	2

APPENDIX 2

A summary of the Subjects Offered to Pupils together with the Constraints on Choice

A2.1 Banbury School Cohort 3

Pupils must choose one subject from each of the columns shown. In addition they study Mathematics, English, Games and a core of short courses. The core consists of 10 week courses in Health Education, RE, PE, Careers and Music/Library. All courses, except Maths, English and Games (1 hour 20 mins per week in one session) and Core (1 hour per week in one session) take place on two occasions each week. One session is 1 hour long and the other 1 hour 20 minutes. Maths and English take place 3 times per week (1 hour session and two 40 minute sessions). All courses, except the core, are two year courses.

All pupils must take at least one Science subject and at least one Human Study. They must also take one subject from the Design, Music, PE or Drama areas.

Table A2.1 Subjects Offered

French	French	Spanish	Action Projects	Pottery	R.E.	Geography
History	History	Russian	Geography	Technical Drawing	Physics	Aeronautics
Business St	P.E. (Boys)	Latin	Physics	Drawing & Painting	Biology	Music
Drama	Chemistry	Chemistry	Chemistry	Auto Eng.	European Studies	Biology
Chemistry	Drawing & Painting	Biology	Secondary Science	Technical/ Electrical	Computer Studies	Drama
Physics	Printmaking	Secondary Science	English Literature	History	Community Studies	Community Studies
Movement & Dance	Technical Drawing	Health Sci	Health Sci	Homemaking	P.E. (Girls)	Metalwork -
Motor Cycling	Woodwork	Rural Studies	Business St	Rural Studies	Drawing & Painting	Graphics
Community Studies	Metalwork	Fabric Printing	Construction	Outdoor Education	Woodwork	Technical/ Electrical
Geography	Child Care	Technical Draiwng	Child Care	Biology	Metalwork	Auto Eng.
Child Care	Food and Nutrition Health Sci	Auto Eng.	Movement & Dance	Needlework	Technical Drawing	Technical Drawing Drawing & Painting
	Needlework Construction	Technical/ Electrical Construction German		Construction P.E. (Girls) Home Economics	Construction Needlework Creative Craft	Child Care Rural Studies Construction
	Action Projects	Business St. Home Economics				Home Economics

A2.2 Drayton School Cohort 3

All courses are planned as two year courses.
All pupils must take ten courses, (Seven 20-minute modules each).

These must include one from each of the following:-

English	in group A
Mathematics	in group B
Core (containing Health, R.E., Music, Careers, games)	in group C
Human Studies	in group D
Sciences	in group E

and five more courses

These five courses can be taken from groups D, E, G and T. (more than one from each group if necessary).

93

Latin and German can only be taken if they were already being studied in the 3rd year.

Construction is a double option (14 modules) and is taken at the Technical College.

Table A2.3 Subject Offered

Group A	**Group G**
English	French 'O'
English	French 'C'
English	European Studies 'C'
English	German 'O/C'
English	Latin 'O'
English	English Literature 'O'
Group B	Cultural Studies 'C' Mode III
Maths	Music 'O'
Maths	Music 'C'
Maths	Drama 'C' Mode III
Maths	Auto Engineering 'C' Mode III
Maths	Technical Drawing 'O/C'
Maths	Metalwork 'C'
Group C	Woodwork 'C' Mode III
Core Subjects N	General Workshop Practice N
Health, Music	Home Economics 'O'
R.E., Careers	Home Economics 'C'
Games	Home Making 'C' Mode III
Group D	Child Care 'C'
History 'O' Mode III	Needlework 'O/C'
History 'C' Mode III	Drawing & Painting 'O/C'
Geography 'O/C'	P.E. (Boys) N
Religious Educ. 'O/C'	Dance (Girls) N
Group E	Business Practice 'O/C'
Physics 'O'	Construction C NOTC
Physics 'C'	
Chemistry 'O'	**Key** O = 'O' level G.C.E.
Chemistry 'C'	C = C.S.E.
Biology 'O'	N = Non-exam
Biology 'C'	NOTC = North Oxon Technical College
Science I (boys) C/N	
Science II (girls) C/N	
General Science N	

A2.3 Drayton School Cohort 4

All courses are planned as two year courses.

Courses A and B	comprise eight 20 minute modules each week.
Course A/B	comprises sixteen 20 minute modules each week.
Course C	comprises two 20 minute modules of Core subjects taken in rotation and four 20 minute modules of games each week.
Courses D, E, F	comprise seven 20 minute module each week.

All pupils must take ten courses. These must include one from each of the following:

English	in Group A ⎱ *or* the double option A/B
Maths	in Group B ⎰
Core	in Group C
Human Studies	in Group D
Sciences	in Group E

and five more courses.

These five courses can be taken from groups D, E and F (more than one from each group if necessary).

Spanish and German can only be taken if they were already being studied in the 3rd year.

General Studies (A/B) takes sixteen modules.

Pupils opting for practical courses must undertake to provide the necessary materials (where appropriate) or be prepared to purchase any articles made during the courses.

Table A2.2 Subjects Offered

GROUP A O/C/N	**GROUP F**
English	French 'O'
English	French 'C'
English	German 'O/C'
English	Spanish 'O/C'
English	European Studies C/N
English	English Literature 'O'
GROUP B O/C/N	Cultural Studies C/N
Maths	Music 'O'
Maths	Music 'C'
Maths	Drama 'C' Mode III
Maths	Music & Drama N
Maths	Auto Engineering 'C'
Maths	Technical Drawing 'O/C'
GROUP C	Metalwork C/N
Core subjects N	Woodwork C/N
Health Education, R.E.	General Workshop Practice N
Music, Careers, Games	Homemaking N
GROUP D	Homemaking 'C'
History 'O'	Home Economics 'C'
History 'C' Mode I	Food & Nutrition 'O'
History 'C' Mode III	Child Care C/N
Geography 'O/C'	Needlework 'O/C
Religious Education 'O/C'	Needlework N
GROUP E	Drawing & Painting O/C/N
Physics 'O' (Nuffield)	Boys' P.E. C/N
Physics 'C'	Girls' P.E. N
Chemistry 'O'	Business Studies 'O'
Chemistry 'C'	Business Practice 'C'
Biology 'O'	Shorthand
Biology 'C'	
Science I (boys) C/N	
Science II (girls) C/N	Key O = 'O' level G.C.E.
General Science N	C = C.S.E.
	N = Non-exam

95

APPENDIX 3

Entry Data Cohorts 3 and 4

Table A3.1 Mean VRQ, Maths*, and Socio Economic Group** Scores

Year of Entry	Cohort	Mean VRQ on Entry	Mean Maths on Entry	Mean Soc-Ec Gp on Entry
1972	3	92.33	93.84	3.06
1973	4	93.33	94.41	—

*Socio Economic Group classification by the Registrar General's Scale: Executive (1)—Manual (5)
*Maths test used was 'Basic Mathematics Test DE (NFER)'

These low VRQ scores on entry do not appear to be peculiar to Banbury; similar results have been found by Thompson at Coventry (Organisation in the Comprehensive School PhD 1973 Leicester). A re-test of VRQ at the end of year one showed means of 100.8 (C3) and 100.9 (C4).

Table A3.2 Allocation to Halls Cohort 3

Year of Entry	Hall	Mean VRQ(N)	Mean Maths/S.D. (N)	Mean Soc-Ec Gp/SD (N)
1972 (C3)	Br	91.86 (105)	94.22/13.76 (113)	3.00/0.81 (111)
	Wy	93.59 (107)	93.61/10.11 (109)	3.00/0.78 (104)
	St	91.63 (106)	93.37/14.93 (111)	3.15/0.72 (108)
	Gr	92.23 (132)	94.09/12.68 (134)	3.06/0.72 (121)

None of the means in any of the columns shown above is significantly different from any other mean in that column.

These tables are compiled from those in Chapter Two of the first phase report.

Appendix 4

Basic Tables for Friendship Pattern Analysis

The tables show the numbers of friends whose VRQ (or attitude scores fall in the particular cells eg. in Table A4.1 11 students in VRQ range 4 had friends in VRQ range 2. Because of the way the data was collected all tables are symmetrical so only one half is shown.

A4.1 ALL FRIENDS

A4.1.1 VRQ

Table A4.1

B+W	1	2	3	4	5	6
1	0					
2	1	2				
3	0	8	4			
4	1	11	20	13		
5	0	3	14	13	9	
6	0	2	7	8	13	3

Table A4.2

S+D	1	2	3	4	5	6
1	1					
2	5	3				
3	1	14	18			
4	2	11	25	15		
5	1	1	9	20	6	
6	0	3	11	9	19	3

A4.1.2 Attitude Scales ABCF & G

Table A4.3

B+W	1	2	3	4	5	6
1	0					
2	0	0				
3	4	4	6			
4	2	4	23	14		
5	1	1	13	29	9	
6	0	0	0	1	2	0

Table A4.4

S+D	1	2	3	4	5	6
1	0					
2	1	2				
3	0	9	13			
4	0	16	21	20		
5	0	2	5	11	5	
6	0	0	2	1	1	0

A4.1.3 Attitude Scales D & E

Table A4.5

B+W	1	2	3	4	5	6
1	2					
2	2	0				
3	4	5	7			
4	0	0	0	0		
5	3	1	22	0	28	
6	1	1	10	0	23	4

Table A4.6

S+D	1	2	3	4	5	6
1	0					
2	1	3				
3	2	10	11			
4	0	0	0	0		
5	1	3	20	0	12	
6	1	4	8	0	15	9

A4.1.4 Attitude Scales H&J

Table A4.7

B+W	1	2	3	4	5	6
1	0					
2	0	1				
3	0	4	9			
4	0	8	12	5		
5	0	6	19	28	17	
6	0	0	0	0	0	0

Table A4.8

S+D	1	2	3	4	5	6
1	0					
2	0	5				
3	0	7	7			
4	0	6	16	18		
5	0	7	11	23	8	
6	0	0	0	0	0	0

A4.1.5 Socio-Economic Group

Table A4.9

B+W	1	2	3	4	5
1	0				
2	3	3			
3	4	22	29		
4	1	8	20	8	
5	0	2	3	0	0

Table A4.10

S+D	1	2	3	4	5
1	0				
2	1	0			
3	3	13	29		
4	2	7	34	12	
5	0	0	1	0	0

A4.1.6 ASI Attitude Scale

Table A4.11

B+W	1	2	3	4	5	6
1	0					
2	0	1				
3	0	7	5			
4	0	5	12	20		
5	0	3	10	12	6	
6	0	0	6	1	4	1

Table A4.12

S	1	2	3	4	5	6
1	0					
2	2	4				
3	1	15	6			
4	0	4	7	4		
5	0	6	4	13	0	
6	0	0	0	0	0	0

A4.2 STRONG FRIENDS ONLY

A4.2.1 VRQ

Table A4.13

B+W	1	2	3	4	5	6
1	0					
2	0	0				
3	0	1	0			
4	0	1	6	2		
5	0	0	3	4	1	
6	0	1	2	1	1	0

Table A4.14

S+D	1	2	3	4	5	6
1	1					
2	1	1				
3	0	8	4			
4	0	1	4	6		
5	0	0	0	8	4	
6	0	0	0	0	0	0

A4.2.2 Attitude Scales ABCF & G

Table A4.15

B+W	1	2	3	4	5	6
1	0					
2	0	0				
3	1	0	2			
4	1	0	5	5		
5	1	0	2	4	3	
6	0	0	0	0	1	0

Table A4.16

S+D	1	2	3	4	5	6
1	0					
2	1	0				
3	0	3	6			
4	0	6	7	7		
5	0	0	3	2	1	
6	0	0	1	1	0	0

A4.2.3 Attitude Scales D & E

Table A4.17

B+W	1	2	3	4	5	6
1	1					
2	0	0				
3	2	0	2			
4	1	0	3	5		
5	0	0	3	6	2	
6	0	0	0	0	0	0

Table A4.18

S+D	1	2	3	4	5	6
1	1					
2	0	0				
3	0	4	5			
4	0	1	8	2		
5	0	1	3	8	4	
6	0	0	0	0	0	0

A4.2.4 Attitude Scales H & J

Table A4.19

B+W	1	2	3	4	5	6
1	1					
2	0	0				
3	2	0	2			
4	1	0	3	5		
5	0	0	3	6	2	
6	0	0	0	0	0	0

Table A4.20

S+D	1	2	3	4	5	6
1	0					
2	0	0				
3	0	4	3			
4	0	0	2	14		
5	0	3	1	8	3	
6	0	0	0	0	0	0

A2.2.5 Socio-Economic Group

Table A4.21

B+W	1	2	3	4	5
1	0				
2	0	2			
3	1	6	7		
4	0	3	3	0	
5	0	1	0	0	0

Table A4.22

S+D	1	2	3	4	5
1	0				
2	1	0			
3	2	5	8		
4	0	1	9	3	
5	0	0	0	0	0

APPENDIX 5

Differential Aptitude Tests

Readers who wish to explore this test battery in detail are refered to the official manual by Bennett, *et al*[1]. We give here a brief introduction to the tests together with one interesting possible application of them.

The tests were developed in America in 1947 as an 'integrated, scientific and well-standardised procedure for measuring the abilities of boys and girls in Grades 8 through 12 for purposes of educational and vocational guidance'.

As aptitude tests they were designed to measure 'condition or sets of characteristics regarded as symptomatic of an individual's ability to acquire with training some (usually specified) knowledge . . .'[2] Thus, as the authors of the manual put it, they measure 'capacity to learn'.

There are eight separate scales in the test battery. Results on two scales are combined to produce a ninth aptitude scale.

The scales are:

Verbal Reasoning	—a measure of the ability to understand concepts which are expressed in words.
Numerical Ability	—this test assesses the understanding of numerical relationships and facility in handling numerical concepts.
Abstract Reasoning	—a non-verbal measure of reasoning ability.
Clerical Speed and Accuracy	—measure the speed of response on a simple task.
Mechanical Reasoning	—measures the ability to understand simple frequently encountered mechanisms which are presented in terms of pictures.
Space Relations	—measure the ability for the mental manipulation of three dimensional objects and the ability to mentally construct such objects from a two dimensional pattern.
Spelling	—spelling.
Language Usage	—measures the ability to detect errors in grammar, punctuation and the use of upper case letters.

Verbal Reasoning and Numerical Ability scores are combined to form the ninth scale which can be thought of as a measure of general scholastic ability.

In view of the purpose for which these tests were constructed and of the results of Chapter 6 of this study (which showed low levels of accuracy in the prognosis made by staff on students) we decided to investigate the possibility of using Differential Aptitude scores to supplement prognosis data. Some correlations between these scores and the results of subject based tests were known for students in America (see Bennett, Seashore and Wesman *op cit*) but these could not easily be related to examination results in this country. We therefore used the data collected by this study to provide equations which could be used to predict examination results from the Differential Aptitude Test scores. The technique used to generate these prediction equations was that of Multiple Regression Analysis. Computer programmes for this were found in the SPSS package which is available on the Oxford University computer. The general interpretation of the statistics produced by this analysis is

---

[1] Bennett, C. K., Seashore, H. G. and Wesman, A. G. *5th Manual for the Differential Aptitude Tests* The Psychological Corporation.

[2] Warren "*Dictionary of Psychology*".

discussed in Chapter 8 of this report, though the reader who requires a more complete understanding is referred to the SPSS manual[1].

The results of the analysis for the 'basic' eight subjects are shown in Table A5.1. An example of a prediction equation is given below:

For Broughton+Wykham O-level chemists . . .

Predicted O-level score[2]$=0.042\times$(SR score)$+0.039\times$(VR score)$+0.865$

Expected error in prediction 0.82

The point of interest in this initial investigation is that prediction equations can be found for most subjects and that, in many cases, they predict examination results to an accuracy of approximately ± 1 grade (See the values of the standard error in the penultimate column of the table.). These levels of accuracy could almost certainly be raised if extra variables (eg. subject preference, subject attainment results attitude to school etc.) were included in the analysis.

It is interesting to note that a second analysis, to try to predict the percentage chance that a student will *choose* a particular subject, failed to produce reliable prediction equations from Differential Aptitude Test scores. (Expected errors in the prediction were usually greater than 40%.)

The implications of these two pieces of work are first, that DAT result do seem to be capable of providing reliable predictors of examination grades, and secondly, that they are not at present strongly related to the issue of subject choice.

If the prediction function can be investigated in depth (and our study is only an initial approach to the subject) we feel that it may well be possible to provide counsellors with more accurate predictions of success than can be done through prognosis at present, and that with this information readily to hand, more appropriate subject choices may be encouraged. There is every possibility of a genuine advantage to individual students from the outcome of work in this area, and we feel that there is every indication that additional work should be made possible.

---

[1] Nie Bent and Hull *Statistical Package for the Social Sciences* McGraw Hill 1970

[2] A score of 6 implies an O level grade of A, 5=B, 4=C, 3=D, 2=E, 1=F.

In CSE predictions a score of 6 implies a grade 1, 5 a grade 2 etc.

Table A5.1 Prediction Equation Variables Relating Examination Success to Differential Aptitude Test Scores

Subject	Variable	B	β	F	Variable	B	β	F	Variable	B	β	F	Const	Standard Error	Percent. Variance
O Level															
English															
S+D	LU	0.066	0.464	18.1	SP	0.023	0.295	7.3					0.022	0.768	42.8
B+W	VR	0.066	0.531	17.7									1.875	0.856	28.2
Maths															
S+D	VN	0.043	0.435	10.0									0.562	0.910	18.9
B+W	SR	0.044	0.443	10.7									2.140	0.907	19.6
Geog.															
S+D	LU	0.171	0.512	15.9	NA	0.113	0.339	6.94					−4.753	1.543	43.6
B+W	no reliable predictor (LU, B = 0.056 standard error in B = 0.039 total % variance 6%)														
History															
S+D	VR	0.097	0.388	5.85	VR	0.086	0.389	4.3					−0.202	1.871	15.1
B+W	MR	−0.076	−0.420	5.1									4.637	1.868	18.4
French															
S+D	LU	0.056	0.452	9.04	VR	0.071	0.571	10.9	SR	−0.036	−0.434	8.2	−1.307	0.718	52.1
B+W	LU	0.151	0.531	13.4									−3.226	1.719	28.2
Physics															
S+D	VN	0.051	0.660	23.9									0.399	0.763	43.6
B+W	MR	0.117	0.529	11.2									−2.344	1.72	27.9
Chem.															
S+D	VN	0.042	0.507	9.4	VR	0.039	0.313	4.4					0.674	0.877	25.7
B+W	SR	0.042	0.379	6.5									0.865	0.823	35.7
Biology															
S+D	SR	0.025	0.311	4.5	LU	0.043	0.301	4.2					1.447	0.870	27.6
B+W	LU	0.058	0.465	10.5									1.790	0.897	21.6
CSE															
English															
S+D	SP	0.033	0.502	45.6	VN	0.028	0.369	17.7	MR	−0.021	−0.209	7.68	2.039	0.707	51.1
B+W	SP	0.027	0.402	25.3	LU	0.040	0.282	12.4					1.708	0.830	32.2
Maths															
S+D	VN	0.040	0.440	20.5	AR	0.067	0.337	12.1	AR	−0.033	−0.297	4.3	−0.148	0.766	42.9
B+W	MR	0.047	0.427	10.0	VN	0.046	0.463	10.6					1.167	0.799	40.1
Geog.															
S+D	VN	0.030	0.396	17.8	LU	0.031	0.246	6.88					1.103	0.828	32.5
B+W	VN	0.035	0.494	32.1									2.656	0.873	24.5
History															
S+D	LU	0.041	0.324	10.8	SP	0.013	0.210	4.5					1.263	0.893	21.7
B+W	VR	0.094	0.378	12.1	MR	0.057	0.230	4.5					−1.285	1.738	26.0
French															
S+D	LU	0.062	0.433	10.3	NA	0.078	0.392	8.4					0.847	0.749	47.0
B+W	no reliable predictor (M.R. B = 0.02 standard error in B = 0.02 % variance = 6%)														
Physics															
S+D	SR	0.064	0.572	15.1									1.030	0.833	32.7
	VN	0.050	0.654	22.4									1.836	0.769	42.7
Chem.															
S+D	SP	0.029	0.501	7.3									2.057	0.885	25.0
B+W	VR	0.073	0.659	27.7									0.948	0.762	43.5
Biology															
S+D	NA	0.100	0.601	24.3									2.698	0.808	36.1
B+W	CS	0.035	0.354	6.03	SR	0.032	0.323	4.99					1.501	0.860	29.8

APPENDIX 6

Subject Choice—basic data

A6.1 Discussion

In this set of tables we offer the basic information on which the subject choice analysis were based.

Tables A6.0 to A6.3 deal with Cohort 3 at Banbury School. Tables A6.4 to A6.7 are the corresponding tables for Cohorts 3 and 4 at Drayton School.

The data for these tables was produced by computer from a basic file of pupils' subject choice and VRQ. The pupils code numbers contain hall and sex information and were used to ensure that each individual's programme was included in the appropriate totals.

Some additional information was extracted from the file for the analysis presented in the later part of Chapter 3 (eg. analysis in 6 VRQ ranges and VRQ analysis for boys and girls seperately). In the interests of conciseness these figures are not given below.

A6.2 Tables

Banbury School

Table A6.0 Total numbers in each Hall; Cohort 3

Hall	Total No.	All Boys	All Girls	Boys + Girls High VRQ	Mid VRQ	Low VRQ
B	71	44	27	21	41	9
W	95	43	52	21	55	19
S	82	35	47	16	46	20

High VRQ = above 110   Mid VRQ = 86-109   Low VRQ = below 85

Table A6.1 Numbers Choosing Individual Subjects Cohort 3

Subject	Hall B	W	S	Subject	Hall B	W	S
Biology	38	43	43	P.E.	17	26	8
Chemistry	36	48	31	Dance	2	12	4
Physics	34	35	27	Home Economics	7	13	8
Rural Studies	8	19	12	Pottery	3	1	4
Health Sci	10	26	16	Drawing & Painting	8	26	18
Secondary Sci	12	18	12	Construction	7	6	11
French	21	38	42	Food & Nutrition	10	5	4
German	8	11	11	Home making	3	7	7
Latin	4	5	1	Technical Drawing	7	13	13
Russian	4	7	4	Auto Eng	13	19	11
Spanish	1	4	3	Technical/Electrical	16	7	4
European Studies	10	10	12	Graphics	1	3	4
				Metalwork	4	4	8
Geography	56	76	73	Woodwork	7	10	3
History	45	54	61	Child Care	13	20	21
R.E.	5	16	4	Needlework	11	9	5
English Literature	8	7	10	Computer Studies	7	13	2
Drama	9	10	14				
Music	7	5	3				

Table A6.2 Numbers choosing at least one subject from a subject group; Cohort 3

Subject Group	Hall B	W	S
Science	All pupils take at least one science		
Human Studies	All pupils take at least one Human Study		
Languages	35	56	55
Design	61	90	73
PE/Dance	18	36	12

Table A6.3 Numbers making specified number of choices from each subject group; Cohort 3

Subject Group	Hall B	W	S	Low VRQ B	W	S	Mid VRQ B	W	S	High VRQ B	W	S	Boys Only B	W	S
SCIENCE															
1 Science	20	22	36	6	6	11	12	14	22	2	2	3	11	8	9
2 Sciences	35	52	33	2	11	9	24	24	16	9	8	8	24	20	17
3 Sciences	16	21	13	1	2	0	5	8	8	10	11	5	9	15	9
LANGUAGES															
No Languages	36	39	27	8	12	13	25	23	13	3	4	1	24	23	19
1 Language	22	37	37	1	5	6	12	23	26	9	9	5	11	13	10
2 Languages	13	19	18	0	2	1	4	9	7	9	8	10	9	7	6
DESIGN															
1 Design	25	44	30	0	3	4	14	24	17	11	17	9	13	20	9
2 Design	20	27	31	3	7	10	13	17	19	4	3	2	12	7	12
3 Design	11	17	8	3	8	3	7	8	5	1	1	0	8	12	7
4 Design	4	2	3	2	0	2	2	2	1	0	0	0	4	2	3
HUMAN STUDIES															
1 Human Study	38	44	28	4	9	8	22	24	14	12	11	6	26	21	15
2 Human Studies	31	45	52	4	8	10	18	29	32	9	8	10	18	20	19
3 Human Studies	2	4	2	1	1	2	1	2	0	0	1	0	0	1	1

Drayton School

Table A6.4 Total number in the streamed and mixed ability cohorts (Cohort 3 and Cohort 4 respectively)

Cohort	Total No	All Boys	All Girls	Boys and Girls High VRQ	Mid VRQ	Low VRQ
C3 (Streamed)	141	79	62	24	91	26
C4 (mixed ability)	138	73	65	7	138	38

Table A6.5 Numbers Choosing Particular Subjects

Subject	C3	C4	Subject	C3	C4
Biology	74	79	Home Economics	22	20
Chemistry	41	65	Homemaking	13	11
Physics	53	49	Metalwork	29	24
Secondary Science	25	19	Technical Drawing	35	34
Health Science	25	31	Woodwork	18	26
French	53	31	Art	47	30
German	17	7	Auto Engineering	15	15
Latin	13	0	Child Care	31	34
European Studies	52	48	General Workshop Practice	17	11
Geography	86	100	Needlework	7	14
History	111	101	Shorthand	13	19
R.E.	25	8	Business Studies	46	61
Cultural Studies	50	9	Drama	12	34
Music	12	17	P.E.	32	46

Table A6.6 Numbers choosing at least one subject from a subject group

Subject Group	C3	C4
Sciences	All pupils take at least one science	
Human Studies	All pupils take at least one Human Study	
Languages	102	83
Design	122	118
PE/Dance	32	46

Table A6.7 Numbers making specified number of choices from each subject

Subject Group	C3	C4	Low VRQ C3	Low VRQ C4	Mid VRQ C3	Mid VRQ C4	High VRQ C3	High VRQ C4	Boys Only C3	Boys Only C4
SCIENCE										
1 Science	75	52	17	25	48	26	10	1	29	20
2 Sciences	40	64	8	10	27	50	5	4	32	39
3 Sciences	22	21	0	3	14	16	8	2	17	14
LANGUAGES										
No Language	39	55	12	13	26	42	1	0	27	33
1 Language	69	67	14	25	51	37	4	5	37	36
2 Languages	33	16	0	0	14	14	19	2	15	4
DESIGN										
1 Design	40	41	4	8	24	29	12	4	21	18
2 Design	56	53	8	18	43	34	5	1	26	28
3 Design	26	24	12	11	14	13	0	0	18	17
HUMAN STUDIES										
1 Human Study	37	57	7	16	26	39	4	2	8	24
2 Human Studies	76	79	15	22	44	53	17	4	46	48
3 Human Studies	25	1	3	0	19	1	3	0	14	0

APPENDIX 7

Composition of Subject Groupings used in the subject choice analysis

Subject Group	YEAR 3	YEAR 4
Science	Biology Chemistry Physics Secondary Science	Biology Chemistry Physics Secondary Science Health Science Rural Studies
Languages	French *German *Spanish *Russian *Latin	French German Spanish Russian Latin European Studies
Human Studies	Geography History R.E.	Geography History R.E.
Maths	Maths	Maths Computer Studies
English	English	English English Literature Drama
P.E.	P.E. Games	P.E. Games Dance
Design	Woodwork Metalwork Needlework Art Home Economics	Woodwork Metalwork Needlework Art Home Economics Graphics Technical Drawing Pottery Homemaking Child Care Auto Engineering Construction Technical/ Electrical Studies Food & Nutrition
Music	Music	Music
Others		Business Studies Community Studies Aeronautics Outdoor Education Film/Roadcraft/ Action Projects/ Community Studies package (FRACS)

*In year three these were available as subjects to be taken outside the timetable.

APPENDIX 8

Career Aspiration

Analysis of separate VRQ ranges

Hall	Sci Ch Non	Soc Ch Non	C/S Ch Non	Lit Ch Non	Art Ch Non	Comp Ch Non	Prac Ch Non	Outdoor Ch Non
LOW VRQ								
B+W	9 28	5 22	9 28	1 36	10 27	3 34	17 20	17 20
S	7 9	6 10	4 12	2 14	5 11	1 15	5 11	6 10
Sig.	NS	NS	NS	NS	NS	NS	NS	NS
Fisher	.95	.54	.66	.21	.74	.65	.24	.39
MID VRQ								
B+W	24 72	28 68	34 62	10 86	34 62	13 83	27 69	34 62
S	14 26	15 25	13 27	4 36	9 31	7 33	13 27	12 28
Sig.	NS	NS	NS	NS	NS	NS	NS	NS
(Chi²)	.95	.56	.01	.05	1.62	.11	.09	.16
HIGH VRQ								
B+W	16 26	9 33	6 36	3 39	13 29	21 21	11 31	12 30
S	5 7	3 9	3 9	3 9	3 9	4 8	2 10	3 9
Sig.	NS	NS	NS	NS	NS	NS	NS	NS
Fisher	.71	.75	.90	.98	.49	.24	.39	.56

Ch = number of pupils putting specified category 1st or 2nd

Non = number of pupils who do not put this category 1st or 2nd

APPENDIX 9

Berrymoor Pupils, Grouping System Differences on Differential Aptitude—Spelling

Table A9.1 Numbers in each Aptitude Range

TEST: SP	Below 25th %tile	25-50th %tile	Above 50th %tile	All Aptitudes
DATA				
Br+Wy	26	17	11	54
St+Dr	9	12	14	35
Totals	35	29	25	89
EXPECTED VALUES FOR SAME ROW & COLUMN TOTALS				
Br+Wy	21.2	17.6	15.2	54.0
St+Dr	13.8	11.4	9.8	35.0
Totals	35.0	29.0	25.0	89.0

Chi squared = 5.682
Degrees of freedom = 2
Significance = 10%

Note that from St+Dr far fewer pupils than expected fall in the lowest aptitude range and rather more in the higher aptitude ranges, especially the top range.

This could be the result of counselling on the basis of traditional academic skills in the streamed system which picks out poor spellers as less able pupils and, in accordance with entry policy, deflects such pupils away from Berrymoor. See the similar indication in Table 3.20 in the main text where it is shown that fewer lower ability streamed pupils go to Berrymoor.

APPENDIX 10

Actual Career Choices of Fifth Year Leavers—Listed under A.P.U. Headings

Table A10.1 Numbers choosing careers in each category

Hall	Sci	Soc	Cl/Sales	Lit	Art	Comp	Prac	Outdoor
B	0	0	7	0	1	2	9	4
W	0	1	5	0	0	0	18	4
S	0	0	7	0	0	0	10	3

We feel sure that the 'Practical' category contains some numbers which, if job specification, rather than just employer were known, would be transfered to other categories.

It is interesting to note that the mean VRQs of pupils prefering the categories Cl/Sales, Practical and Outdoor were, respectively 94.5, 96.9 and 98.1 for Br+Wy pupils and 97.1, 95.9 and 95.3 for St. This should be compared with the mean VRQs for those leaving school of 98.2 (Br+Wy) and 91 (St). The higher mean VRQs of those prefering the Science, Literature and Computational categories (See Table 5.6) might explain the low numbers of *actual* leavers who take up careers in these areas. (*ie.* the leavers are lower VRQ pupils, while those showing a preference for these areas, are higher VRQ pupils). If such an explanation is accepted the very low numbers taking up 'Social' category jobs, is interesting (since the mean VRQ of those who prefer this category is low and the numbers prefering it are high). This could be the result of job availability in the Banbury area, or of the fact that the pupils were not asked to assess their ability to do a job when selecting the areas in which they would prefer to work. The preference results in Table 5.4 may therefore show a large number of people who would like to work in jobs in the 'Social' category but who are not suitable to do so. This lack of suitability for their preferred job area might also explain the low numbers actually taking up jobs in the 'Outdoor' category.

APPENDIX 11

Pupils' Sixth Form Choice VRQ ranges of those choosing particular subjects

Subjects	Broughton+Wykham		Stanbridge+Drayton		Fisher Test between systems	Significance of difference between systems
	No. Above VRQ 116	No. Below VRQ 116	No. above VRQ 116	No. Below VRQ 116		
Biology	6	8	5	4	.4334	NS
Chemistry	7	12	4	6	.7170	NS
Physics	4	7	4	5	.7951	NS
Maths	9	10	5	2	.2609	NS
English	4	8	3	15	.2665	NS
Geography	3	4	3	10	.3359	NS
History	3	5	2	6	.5000	NS

If the extra pupils choosing, for example, sciences were in some way less suiatble pupils for the courses, we would expect, from the system which supplied the extra pupils, a larger number in the below 116 VRQ range. Since this never happens we conclude that the grouping system difference shown in Table 5.8 was not due to unrealistic choices from pupils in one or other of the grouping systems.

Attitude Measurement—Details of the Instruments used

A12.1 Questions Set

A.S.I.

Scale 1—Pupil participation and integration
 1. A crowd of pupils here never want to come to school socials.
 2. Pupils run some things in this school themselves, without teachers interfering.
 4. You can make your own choice of options here without anyone interfering.
 6. We never get a chance to make our views known in house or school meetings.
 7. We are given a lot of choice about things here.
 8. Pupils here willingly discuss their choice of careers with teachers.
 9. Pupils readily go to teachers for advice about choices they need to make at school.
10. Once a pupil has been given a responsible job here, the teachers let him get on with it.
13. Prefects never handle any difficulties themselves here, but always call in the staff.
15. Pupils here have no say in what goes on in assembly.
19. Other pupils make fun of you if you speak nicely here.
21. If you belong to a school club, you get some say in what activities go on in it.
22. There are plenty of school societies to choose from.
24. Pupils have a lot to do with planning school socials.
25. If there are several activities going on as part of a lesson, you can choose which one you will take part in.

Subject Choice Satisfaction Scale
 1. Most of the subjects I chose turned out to be a bit boring.
 2. I didn't know what I was letting myself in for with some of the subjects I chose.
 3. I thought I would like the subjects I chose but I don't.
 4. I seem to be getting on well in the subjects I chose.
 5. I think the subjects I chose will help me later on.
 6. Even if I had a chance to change now I'd still keep to the subjects I've chosen.
 7. If I could choose again I would choose different subjects.
 8. I'm glad I chose the subjects I did.
 9. I can't really do the work in the subjects I've chosen.
10. I was lucky—I was able to do all the subjects I wanted to.

There are ten items, five negative and five positive scored on a five-point scale with a score range of 10-50.

A12.2 Intercorrelations of ASI Scale 1 which we used with other ASI and NSI (Nature of Social Interaction) scales which could have been used

The measurements, taken from 'A Matter of Choice' were made in four schools which are here presented separately.

	NSI				ASI	
	1	2	3	4	1	2
School A NSI 1	—					
2	.54	—				
3	.45	.70	—			
4	.61	.58	.64	—		
ASI 1	.48	.57	.70	.58	—	
2	.46	.46	.64	.70	.70	—
School B NSI 1	—					
2	.51	—				
3	.46	.67	—			
4	.69	.50	.49	—		
ASI 1	.52	.58	.65	.55		
2	.55	.53	.58	.72	.60	—
School C NSI 1	—					
2	.48	—				
3	.57	.77	—			
4	.66	.65	.69	—		
ASI 1	.56	.69	.67	.67	—	
2	.63	.61	.68	.81	.68	—
School D NSI 1	—					
2	.41	—				
3	.36	.61	—			
4	.67	.40	.44	—		
ASI 1	.37	.46	.59	.39	—	
2	.51	.43	.60	.58	.52	—

APPENDIX 13

The Relationship between Prognosis and Examination Results

Examination grades are A-E and U for O-level and 1-5 and U for CSE. In each case they have been coded as 1-6 with 1 being the best result.

Prognosis has been scored from 1 to 6 with 1 being the best prognosis.

The tables below show the numbers of pupils with particular combinations of exam grade and progonsis.

O-LEVEL EXAMINATIONS

Table A13.1 Broughton Hall

Grade	1	2	3	4	5	6
Prognosis 1	12	13	10	7	6	3
2	11	12	26	19	13	11
3	0	1	3	3	4	2
4	0	1	3	2	3	12
5	0	0	0	0	0	0
6	0	0	0	0	0	0

Table A13.2 Wykham Hall

Grade	1	2	3	4	5	6
Prognosis 1	7	24	14	3	7	2
2	5	25	34	11	11	8
3	0	9	6	2	3	7
4	0	5	6	5	0	1
5	0	0	1	0	0	0
6	0	0	0	0	0	0

Table A13.3 Stanbridge Hall

Grade	1	2	3	4	5	6
Prognosis 1	4	7	11	6	1	0
2	4	20	32	11	17	4
3	0	7	8	4	6	7
4	0	1	6	4	1	6
5	1	0	3	1	1	0
6	0	0	0	0	0	1

CSE EXAMINATIONS

Table A13.4 Broughton Hall

Grade	1	2	3	4	5	6
Prognosis 1	4	2	3	1	0	1
2	5	9	9	7	0	0
3	6	8	7	13	2	1
4	6	31	60	42	14	4
5	1	3	11	11	1	1
6	0	3	4	6	11	4

Table A13.5 Wykham Hall

Grade	1	2	3	4	5	6
Prognosis 1	1	1	3	1	0	0
2	9	10	17	9	5	0
3	4	11	21	21	3	2
4	4	16	41	51	26	7
5	1	1	7	10	8	1
6	1	0	2	13	5	1

Table A13.6 Stanbridge Hall

Grade	1	2	3	4	5	6
Prognosis 1	2	6	4	2	0	0
2	8	13	12	10	2	0
3	6	10	7	9	2	0
4	8	16	53	62	17	2
5	1	3	19	16	20	5
6	0	1	4	8	9	2

APPENDIX 14

A Survey of Ability Differences of Pupils from the two Grouping Systems who were Entered for CSE and O-level Examinations.

The figures here are, for reasons of space, a selection from those which provided the data for the 320 F tests referred to in Section 4.2. They present VRQ data for all subjects at CSE and O-level and full data for those subjects which seemed to show the greatest number of statistically significant differences.

Table A14.1 Mean VRQ scores of those entered at O-level and CSE

Statistic	Maths	English	Geog	Hist	French	Biol	Chem	Physics
Broughton+Wykham O-level								
Mean	114.4	108.1	112.3	110.9	111.1	109.6	111.3	112.9
Stand. Dev.	9.89	10.6	10.6	10.9	21.4	20.8	10.3	10.6
No.	46	47	31	32	36	40	41	31
Stanbridge+Drayton O-level								
Mean	109.1	106.2	110.3	110.2	109.4	107.2	111.3	105.1
Stand. Dev.	18.7	16.7	9.5	10.4	10.6	19.1	10.0	21.4
No.	45	63	38	35	43	46	29	33
F test sig.	**	**	NS	NS	**	NS	NS	**
t test sig.	NS	NS	NS	NS	NS	NS	NS	NS
Broughton+Wykham CSE								
Mean	101.7	90.0	94.6	93.1	107.3	97.9	104.3	102.5
Stand. Dev.	17.5	22.8	24.7	19.1	13.5	19.3	13.4	22.4
No.	49	124	101	77	23	40	38	32
Stanbridge+Drayton CSE								
Mean	101.9	93.6	95.6	92.6	103.7	99.3	102.0	101.1
Stand. Dev.	9.4	14.0	14.6	14.8	10.7	10.5	9.7	9.0
No.	76	131	114	110	37	45	24	33
F test sig.	**	**	**	NS	NS	**	NS	**
t test sig	NS	NS	NS	NS	NS	NS	NS	NS

Table A14.2 Subjects Showing Several Significant Differences

Statistic	VRQ	VR	NA	VN	AR	CS	MR	SR	SP	LU
ENGLISH O-LEVEL										
Broughton+Wykham										
Mean	108.1	30.74	18.2	48.9	37.5	43.3	45.9	35.8	62.7	32.6
Stand. Dev.	10.6	10.0	8.4	16.9	9.5	11.8	12.6	12.8	18.6	8.4
No.	47	47	47	47	47	47	47	47	47	47
Stanbridge+Drayton										
Mean	106.2	27.7	16.0	43.7	34.2	40.8	42.0	31.1	66.4	31.2
Stand. Dev.	16.7	12.2	7.9	18.3	12.4	17.4	16.2	14.8	25.0	12.3
No.	63	63	63	63	63	63	63	63	63	63
F test sig.	**	NS	NS	NS	NS	*	NS	NS	*	*
t test sig.	NS	NS	NS	NS	NS	NS	NS	NS	NS	NS
PHYSICS CSE										
Broughton+Wykham										
Mean	102.5	26.5	16.8	43.3	37.9	44.4	45.0	32.8	59.2	28.7
Stand. Dev.	22.4	8.6	6.8	12.7	4.7	11.8	7.9	10.4	18.9	7.8
No.	32	32	32	32	32	32	32	32	32	32
Stanbridge+Drayton										
Mean	101.1	24.5	13.8	38.3	31.1	39.2	40.4	28.2	55.4	23.9
Stand. Dev.	9.0	10.5	7.0	16.0	11.8	18.8	16.3	12.1	21.8	10.0
No.	33	33	33	33	33	33	33	33	33	33
F test sig.	**	NS	NS	NS	**	**	**	NS	NS	NS
t test sig.	NS	NS	NS	NS	**	NS	NS	NS	NS	*

To complete this 'base line' comparison between systems, we give in Table A14.3 a comparison of the numbers entered for CSE and O-level.

Subject	No. of entries at O-level		No of entries at CSE		Chi-Squared
	B+W	S+D	B+W	S+D	
Maths	46	45	113	131	0.32 NS
English	47	64	124	131	0.99 NS
History	32	35	77	110	0.62 NS
Geography	31	38	101	114	0.02 NS
French	36	43	23	37	0.46 NS
Chemistry	41	29	38	24	0.02 NS
Physics	31	33	32	33	0.01 NS
Biology	40	46	40	45	0.01 NS

Table A.14.3 Numbers of O-level and CSE Entries in the two Grouping Systems

We should note perhaps, that there are several subjects which are only taken at CSE (eg. Rural Studies, Secondary Science, European Studies) and that the figures above cannot therefore be used to infer details of the total number of examination candidates presented by the science and languages subject groups.

We would remind the reader that differences in entry policy would be most unexpected in the Banbury situation because, when entry decisions are made, all pupils are in cross-hall teaching groups. What is more, their entries are administered by the same Head of Department whichever hall they attended in their first four years.

APPENDIX 15

Index to Data Files

The following files have been created during the course of the Banbury Project. Brief details of the file contents are given. The total content of the files represents a unique collection of data concerning a single group of schoolchildren. Many of the files were created for specific purposes and so repetition of various items will be found. It has been thought useful, however, to keep all the various combinations of data. The files are stored on magnetic tape held at the Oxford University Computing Service. File names reflect in some way the type of data to be found. In particular the prefix C3, C4 etc. identify the particular cohort to which the file applies. C3 entered their 5th year in September 1976, C4 in 1977.

FILENAME	BRIEF DETAILS
KEYFILE	Index to all files on the mag-tape.
C3SUBCHOICEN	7 chosen subjects, number coded, + 2 reserve subjects.
C3ASISSWC	Scores on ASI and SSCS tests (ASI = Amount of Social Interaction, SSCS = Student Satisfaction with Course Scale.
ATTC2Y2	Cohort 2 attitude scores (for year 2).
ATTC2Y3	Cohort 2 attitude scores (for year 3).
ATTC3Y2	Cohort 3 attitude scores (for year 2).
C3DIFFAPNM	Differential Aptitude Scores (taken in year 4) Choice of Berrymoor is also indicated.
C3DAPSUBCHV	Contains C3DIFFAPNM and C3SUBCHOICEN
C4DIFFAPP	As C3DIFFAPNM but for Cohort 4 (taken in year 3.)
C3ATTFILER	Scores on Barker Lunn Attitude tests.
C3SUBDRAY	Drayton Subject Choice, number coded 7 choices + English Literature, if appropriate.
C3PROGFILEA	Code + Prognosis results on 17 subjects.
C3SUBDRAYV	A C3SUBDRAY but including VRQ
C4Y1Y2FREN	Code numbers of 4 friends. Taken in years 1 and 2. For Cohort 4.
C2Y1Y2Y3FREN	As above. Cohort 2, years 1-3.
C5Y1	Entry data (eg. date of birth, Primary School, VRQ, Reading Age).
C3PROGRES	Prognosis, Subject Choice and Exam results.
C3PROGNOSE	Full Prognosis scores (inverted)
C3DAPSUBRES	VRQ, DAT[1] Score, Subject Choice and results.
C3PROGFILE	Prognosis (Inverted) Subject Choice VRQ.
C3DAPSUBCHV	DAT scores, Subject Choice, Attitudes VRQ.
C3ATTFILE	Barker Lunn Attitude Scores
C4SUBDRAY	Subject Choice number coded.
C4Y1Y2	Entry Data (eg. VRQ, Attitudes, Reading Ages).
C1YR1	Attitude Scores Cohort 1
C34Y1Y2	As for C4Y1Y2 but including Cohort 3 students
C3SIXSUB	6th form Choice of Subject number coded.
C3VRQ	VRQ Scores.
C3FRENYRI23	Students' Friends over three years.
C3FRENSPECDR	Entry data together with 4th year friendship group Drayton Students.
C3SUBCHON	Code numbers with Subject Choice.
C3SUBTEMP	Subject Choice & DAT Scores
C3RESULTS	ASI Score, Soc-Ec Gp. Attitudes VRQ and subject results at 'O' and CSE.

---

[1] DAT=Differential Aptitude Test

FILENAME	BRIEF DETAILS
C3RESULTS1	As above with Subject Choice codes.
C3PROG	Prognosis (Not inverted).
C3ASISSAV	ASI Score, SSCS score, Soc-Ec Gp., Attitudes VRQ
C30CSE	Subject Results at 'O' or CSE, VRQ range.
C3FRENSPEC1	As C3FRENSPECDR, Banbury School Students.
ATTC3Y2MORE	Attitudes.
C3CHOICE	Choice of school, career or tech. at 16+ 6th form Subject Choice.
C3FRENGPNOS	Nos in Friendship Groups in order of C3Y1Y2Y3.
C3SUBFRAR	File is arranged in friendship groups, showing subject choice with friendship group number.
STAFF99	Staff questionaire results.
C2Y1Y2Y3	Test scores on entry, VRQ, Soc. Ec. Gp, Primary School, Attitudes, Name.
C3Y1Y2Y3	As above.
ATTC2Y2Y3	Attitude scores.
C3APUV	APU Score, VRQ, Attitudes
C4SUBDRAYV	Subject choice, VRQ.
C3SUBFREN	Subject choice, Friendship group

Keith Postlethwaite was educated at Marling School Stroud and St. Catharine's College Cambridge, where he read Natural Sciences. He joined Banbury School staff in 1971 as a teacher of physics and is now responsible for Statistics and Research in the school.

Cliff Denton was educated at Bassaleg Grammer School, Monmouthshire (now Gwent), served five years as an RAF Coastal Command Pilot and then read Mathematics at Kings College Cambridge. He joined Banbury School in 1974 on the mathematics staff and now takes particular responsibility for Computer Studies.

Previous publications from Pubansco :-
The School as a Centre of Enquiry 1975 (3rd Edition out of print).
Community Sports Coaching 1976 £1.00.

Forthcoming publications :-
Banbury School, Ten Years On
Into Teaching

Copies of Pubansco publications are available from Pubansco, Banbury School, Banbury, Oxon.